Editor
Stephanie Buehler, Psy.D.

Editorial Project Manager
Ina Massler Levin, M.A.

Editor-in-Chief
Sharon Coan, M.S. Ed.

Cover Artist
Jessica Orlando

Art Coordinator
Denice Adorno

Imaging
Alfred Lau
Rosa C. See

Product Manager
Phil Garcia

Publishers
Rachelle Cracchiolo, M.S. Ed.
Mary Dupuy Smith, M.S. Ed.

Descriptive Writing

Grades 6–8

Written by

Rebecca Rozmiarek, M.A.T./M.S.

Teacher Created Materials, Inc.
6421 Industry Way
Westminster, CA 92683
www.teachercreated.com

ISBN-1-57690-997-2

©2000 Teacher Created Materials, Inc.
Reprinted, 2002
Made in U.S.A.

Table of Contents

Table of Contents *(cont.)*

Introduction

Middle school students are at a time in their development when they seek to establish their own identities, which is one reason why descriptive writing has such appeal for them. Descriptive writing allows writers to express the ways in which they view and experience the world. At the same time, many skills can be taught while the students enjoy their attempts at self-expression.

This comprehensive book contains practical step-by-step lessons designed to build skills in such areas as focusing the topic, using graphic organizers, selecting appropriate transitional words, and appealing to the intended audience. There also are writing process connections, student samples, and writing prompts that are ready for immediate classroom use. Scoring rubrics provide clearly defined criteria for evaluating the skills being taught. At the end of the book is a final assessment that incorporates the writing process and determines the students' proficiency in adding various stylistic elements.

Each descriptive writing lesson provides you with objectives, standards for mastery, and the procedure for completing the activities. Each lesson also gives you many ideas for ways to extend the lesson:

- **Portfolio Piece** provides you with ways to get students to reflect on the strengths and weaknesses of their writing.

- **Publishing** prompts you to organize celebrations of student work.

- **Technology Connection** offers ideas for doing research, revising, and enhancing text with graphics and fonts.

- **Home-School Connection** provides ideas for linking what the students are learning in school with their lives outside of school.

- **Assessment** gives you ways to evaluate the students' work and determine if they have achieved mastery.

By completing the lessons in this book, students will learn how to write descriptive paragraphs, essays, stories, and articles for the purpose of entertaining and influencing audiences.

Standards for Writing
Grades 6-8

Accompanying the major activities of this book will be references to the basic standards and benchmarks for writing that will be met by successful performance of the activities. Each specific standard and benchmark will be referred to by the appropriate letter and number from the following collection. For example, a basic standard and benchmark identified as **1A** would be as follows:

> **Standard 1:** Demonstrates competence in the general skills and strategies of the writing process
>
> **Benchmark A:** Prewriting: Uses a variety of prewriting strategies (e.g., makes outlines, uses published pieces as writing models, constructs critical standards, brainstorms, builds background knowledge)

A basic standard and benchmark identified as **4B** would be as follows:

> **Standard 4:** Gathers and uses information for research purposes
>
> **Benchmark B:** Uses the card catalog to locate books for research topics

Clearly, some activities will address more than one standard. Moreover, since there is a rich supply of activities included in this book, some will overlap in the skills they address; and some, of course, will not address every single benchmark within a given standard. Therefore, when you see these standards referenced in the activities, refer to this section for complete descriptions.

Although virtually every state has published its own standards and every subject area maintains its own lists, there is surprising commonality among these various sources. For the purpose of this book, we have elected to use the collection of standards synthesized by John S. Kendall and Robert J. Marzano in their book *Content Knowledge: A Compendium of Standards and Benchmarks for K-12 Education* (Second Edition, 1997) as illustrative of what students at various grade levels should know and be able to do. The book is published jointly by McREL (Mid-continent Regional Educational Laboratory, Inc.) and ASCD (Association for Supervision and Curriculum Development). (Used by permission of McREL.)

Language Arts Standards

1. Demonstrates competence in the general skills and strategies of the writing process

2. Demonstrates competence in the stylistic and rhetorical aspects of writing

3. Uses grammatical and mechanical conventions in written compositions

4. Gathers and uses information for research purposes

Standards for Writing
Grades 6-8 *(cont.)*

---

1. Demonstrates competence in the general skills and strategies of the writing process

    A. Prewriting: Uses a variety of prewriting strategies (e.g., makes outlines, uses published pieces as writing models, constructs critical standards, brainstorms, builds background knowledge)

    B. Drafting and Revising: Uses a variety of strategies to draft and revise written work (e.g., analyzes and clarifies meaning, makes structural and syntactical changes, uses an organizational scheme, uses sensory words and figurative language, rethinks and rewrites for different audiences, and purposes, checks for a consistent point of view and for transitions between paragraphs, uses direct feedback to review compositions)

    C. Editing and Publishing: Uses a variety of strategies to edit and publish written work (e.g., proofreads using reference materials, word processor, and other resources; edits for clarity, word choice, and language usage; uses a word processor to publish written work)

    D. Evaluates own and other's writing (e.g., applies criteria generated by self and others; uses self-assessment to set and achieve goals as a writer; participates in peer response groups)

    E. Uses style and structure appropriate for specific audiences (e.g., public, private) and purposes (e.g., to entertain, to influence, to inform)

    F. Writes expository compositions (e.g., presents information that reflects knowledge about the topic of the report; organizes and presents information in a logical manner)

    G. Writes narrative accounts (e.g., engages the readers by establishing a context and otherwise developing reader interest; establishes a situation, plot, persona, point of view, setting, and conflict; creates an organizational structure that balances and unifies all narrative aspects of the story; uses sensory details and concrete language to develop plot and character; excludes extraneous details and inconsistencies; develops complex characters; uses a range of strategies such as dialogue, tension or suspense, naming, and specific narrative action such as movement, gestures, and expressions)

    H. Writes compositions about autobiographical incidents (e.g., explores the significance and personal importance of the incident; uses details to provide a context for the incident; reveals personal attitude towards the incident; presents details in a logical manner)

    I. Writes biographical sketches (e.g., illustrates the subject's character using narrative and descriptive strategies such as relevant dialogue, specific action, physical description, background description, and comparison or contrast to other people; reveals the significance of the subject to the writer; presents details in a logical manner)

Standards for Writing
Grades 6-8 *(cont.)*

J. Writes persuasive compositions (e.g., engages the reader by establishing a context, creating a persona, and otherwise developing reader interest; develops a controlling idea that conveys a judgment; creates and organizes a structure appropriate to the needs and interests of a specific audience; arranges details, reasons, examples, and/or anecdotes persuasively; excludes information and arguments that are irrelevant; anticipates and addresses reader concerns and counter-arguments; supports arguments with detailed evidence, citing sources of appropriate information)

K. Writes compositions that speculate on problems/solutions (e.g., identifies and defines a problem in a way appropriate to the intended audience, describes at least one solution, presents logical and well-supported reasons)

L. Writes in response to literature (e.g., anticipates and answers a reader's questions, responds to significant issues in a log or journal, answers discussion questions, writes a summary of a book, describes an initial impression of a text, connects knowledge from a text with personal knowledge)

M. Writes business letters and letters of request and response (e.g., uses business letter format; states purpose of the letter; relates opinions, problems, requests, or complaints; uses precise vocabulary)

2. Demonstrates competence in the stylistic and rhetorical aspects of writing

A. Uses descriptive language that clarifies and enhances ideas (e.g., establishes tone and mood, uses figurative language)

B. Uses paragraph form in writing (e.g., arranges sentences in sequential order, uses supporting and follow-up sentences)

C. Uses a variety of sentence structures to express expanded ideas

D. Uses some explicit transitional devices

3. Uses grammatical and mechanical conventions in written compositions

A. Uses simple and compound sentences in written compositions

B. Uses pronouns in written compositions (e.g., relative, demonstrative, personal, possessive, subject, object)

C. Uses nouns in written compositions (e.g., forms possessive nouns, forms irregular plural nouns)

D. Uses verbs in written compositions (e.g., uses linking and auxiliary verbs, verb phrases, and correct forms of regular and irregular verbs)

E. Uses adjectives in written compositions (e.g., pronominal, positive, comparative, superlative)

F. Uses adverbs in written compositions (e.g., chooses between forms of adjectives and adverbs)

Standards for Writing
Grades 6-8 *(cont.)*

G. Uses prepositions and coordinating conjunctions in written compositions (e.g., uses prepositional phrases, combines and embeds ideas using conjunctions)

H. Uses interjections in written compositions

I. Uses conventions of spelling in written compositions (e.g., spells high frequency, commonly misspelled words from appropriate grade-level list, uses a dictionary and other resources to spell words, uses common prefixes and suffixes as aids to spelling, applies rules for irregular structural changes)

J. Uses conventions of capitalization in written compositions (e.g., titles, books, stories, poems, magazines, newspapers, songs, works of art), proper nouns (team names, companies, schools and institutions, departments of government, religions, school subjects), proper adjectives (nationalities, brand names of products)

K. Uses conventions of punctuation in written compositions (e.g., uses exclamation marks after exclamatory sentences and interjections; uses periods in decimals, dollars, and cents; uses commas with nouns of address and after mild interjections; uses quotation marks with poems, songs, and chapters; uses colons in business letter salutations; uses hyphens to divide words between syllables at the end of a line)

L. Uses standard format in written compositions (e.g., includes footnotes, uses italics for titles of books, magazines, plays, and movies)

4. Gathers and uses information for research purposes

A. Gathers data for research topics from interviews (e.g., prepares and asks relevant questions, makes notes of responses; compiles responses)

B. Uses the card catalog to locate books for research topics

C. Uses the *Readers' Guide to Periodical Literature* and other indexes to gather information for research topics

D. Uses a computer catalog to gather information for research topics

E. Uses a variety of resource materials to gather information for research topics (e.g., magazines, newspapers, dictionaries, schedules, journals, phone directories, globes, atlases, almanacs)

F. Determines the appropriateness of an information source for a research topic

G. Organizes information and ideas from multiple sources in systematic ways (e.g., time lines, outlines, notes, graphic representations)

H. Writes research papers (e.g., separates information into major components based on a set of criteria, examines critical relationships between and among elements of a research topic, integrates a variety of information into a whole)

Standards and Benchmarks: 1A, 1B, 1C, 1D, 1E, 1G, 1I, 2A

Criteria of Descriptive Writing

Objective: The students will identify the criteria of descriptive writing in a sample piece and then write their own pieces of descriptive writing.

Procedure

1. Write a definition of descriptive writing on the overhead or chalkboard: Descriptive writing uses adequate details to describe a particular topic in such a way as to appeal to the audience.

2. Inform the students that descriptive writing has the following criteria:
   - a focused topic
   - an engaging lead
   - adequate supporting details
   - transitions
   - varied sentence structure and length
   - several elements of stylistic language (similes, metaphors, adjectives, etc.)
   - a powerful conclusion

3. Have students read the sample on page 10 and discuss the criteria met by the piece.

4. Select all or some of the following tasks for the students:
   - Use the lessons throughout this section for instruction.
   - Use the prompts on pages 79–132 for student response.
   - Use the "Descriptive Writing Peer Response Form" on page 13 for the students to give each other feedback.
   - Use the "Descriptive Writing Rubric" (page 14) to give the students an opportunity to evaluate their own writing.

Portfolio Piece: Have students include their descriptive writing in their portfolios. Have them reflect on how they wrote their lead and included strong supporting details.

Publishing: Provide students with the opportunity to publish their descriptive writing in a class anthology.

Technology Connection: Have students word process their descriptive writing to resemble excellent published examples.

Home-School Connection: Share descriptive writing with family members.

Assessment: Use the "Descriptive Writing Rubric" on page 14 to evaluate the students' descriptive writing.

Example of a Description of Setting

Imagine a hot, summer day. The sun beats down on the blacktop and the city air rises up in a zigzag. Light bounces off the cars parked on the street. For a time, the only sound heard throughout the neighborhood is the steady hum of fans, laboring to cool residents from the sweltering temperatures.

Bored children decide to brave the humid heat and play ball in the streets. Thump! Thump! Thump! The repetitive sound of a basketball breaks the monotonous silence. The children weave in and out, in and out, jumping, moving, dodging, and laughing as they move effortlessly, making plays in the hot summer rays.

Spewing a nerve-jangling tune, an ice cream truck arrives on the scene. The kids race over to the truck and select treats—vanilla cones, chocolate crunch bars, wildly colored ice pops. In minutes, the treats are devoured and the kids return to their energetic play.

Dark storm clouds roll through the sky overhead and the street empties. A gloomy grayness envelops the sky like a giant umbrella. Craaaaack! Thunder roars with anger and lightning dances fleetingly in the distance. The rain comes in torrents, beating, beating, beating down on the sidewalks, streets, and houses. Faces peer out windows, watching the dazzling show. When the clouds roll away, steam rises, drying the streets for another round of play.

• • •

Stylistic elements included:

Engaging lead: Imagine a hot, summer day.

Alliteration: humid heat, chocolate crunch

Onomatopoeia: Thump!, Craaaaack!

Repetition: in and out, "-ing" verbs

Vivid verbs: jumping, moving, dodging, laughing, etc.

Simile: A gloomy grayness envelops the sky like a giant umbrella.

Personification: thunder roars with anger; lightning dances fleetingly

Example of a Description of Character

Tall, skinny, imposing—that's how Johnny's friends would describe him. Johnny's dark hair was always slicked back with a bit of gel so that it would stay in place all day. He wore the latest fashion: gigantic T-shirt, baggy shorts, and expensive athletic shoes. What the girls liked best, though, were his sparkling blue eyes that always suggested mischief.

Johnny was a powerhouse on the basketball court, too. Some say he could make a shot from a thousand feet away. His agility enabled him to leap, dodge, and dance down the basketball court. In action, he was a gazelle, moving effortlessly toward his destination. On the court, his friends called him "Jumping Johnny" because as he approached the net, he would soar through the air about 10 feet, SLAM the ball into the net, land on his feet and race down the court for the next play.

At home, "Jumping Johnny" was neither mischievous nor leaping, jumping, and dodging. He helped his little sister with homework, assisted with setting the dinner table, and mowed the lawn every weekend during the summer. He loved history and would spend hours every evening reading about famous battles and former Presidents of the United States. When the phone would ring in the evening, Johnny would talk, laughing and joking about the day's events, knowing that the following day would bring more amazing adventures.

● ● ●

Stylistic elements included:

Repetition of adjectives: tall, skinny, imposing

Specific nouns and descriptive adjectives: dark hair with a bit of gel; gigantic T-shirt; sparkling blue eyes

Hyperbole: Some say he could make a shot from a 1000 feet away.

Metaphor: In action, he was a gazelle, moving effortlessly toward his destination.

Vivid verbs: approached, soar, assisted, leaping, jumping, dodging

Alliteration: Jumping Johnny; amazing adventures

Repetition: -ing verbs

Example of a Description of Action

Have you ever witnessed a scene of such peace and tranquility that its beauty overwhelmed you? Such was the scene of two beautiful deer grazing in the still pasture as twilight approached. Blues, purples, pinks, yellows, and oranges streaked the sky like a magnificent painting. Every few seconds, one of the deer's tails twitched as it lifted its head to look around carefully before returning to its dinner. Dark shadows lengthened as the evening crept closer and closer. The forest that surrounded the pasture seemed to beckon to the deer, urging them to seek refuge from any lurking dangers.

Suddenly from out of the forest, a large fox raced toward the deer. As soon as they sensed movement, the deer took off in opposite directions, at first erratic and confused, then purposeful and focused as they ran as fast as a speeding locomotive attempting to evade their predator. The fox paused. Then, instinctively, it raced after the slower deer, deep into the pine forest. Then, all was quiet again in the pasture. Quiet. Dark. Somehow less peaceful.

The sky quickly became a murky grayish pink. The sky painting appeared as if a bucket of water had spilled across the canvas, washing away the vibrant colors. Two bunnies darted playfully and fireflies flickered repeatedly in the dusk. Within minutes the atmosphere of peace had returned, the skirmish toward death forgotten.

●   ●   ●

Stylistic elements included:

Vivid verbs: grazing, approached, streaked, twitched, lifted, lengthened, crept, beckon, seek, raced, evade, paused, ensued, created, entered, followed, darted, flickered, returned.

Alliteration: tails twitched; fireflies flickered

Assonance: The forest that surrounded the pasture seemed to beckon to the deer, urging them to seek refuge from any lurking dangers.

Simile: The sky painting disappeared as if a bucket of water had spilled across the canvas, washing the vibrant colors away.

Personification: . . .the evening crept closer; The forest . . . seemed to beckon to the deer, urging them to seek refuge from any lurking dangers.

Descriptive Writing Peer Response Form

Writer: _____

Peer Responder: _____

Directions: Writers should read their draft aloud to a peer, then write down the peer's responses to the following questions.

1. What is the topic of my descriptive writing? How could my topic be more focused?

   _____

   _____

   _____

2. How could my lead be more engaging to the reader?

   _____

   _____

3. What are the details in my writing? How could these details more clearly describe my topic?

   _____

   _____

4. What information do I need to add, delete, or change in my conclusion in order to make it more powerful?

   _____

   _____

5. How have I shown an understanding of the audience? Give specific information from the text.

   _____

   _____

6. Which of my transitions is particularly effective? How could I improve my transitions?

   _____

   _____

   _____

7. Do I have varied sentence structure and length? Give specific examples.

   _____

   _____

   _____

Descriptive Writing Rubric

Directions: Use the following rubric to evaluate descriptive writing

I. Elements of Descriptive Writing

	Self	Peer	Teacher
1. The topic is focused. (2)			
2. The lead is engaging and "grabs" the reader. (4)			
3. Supporting details are sufficient. (4)			
4. Conclusion is powerful. (4)			
5. An awareness of audience is evident. (2)			
6. Transitions link ideas. (3)			
7. Sentence structure is varied. (3)			
8. Sentence length is varied. (3)			
Total points out of 25			

II. Writer's Evaluation

My strengths in my writing are _____

_____

_____

_____

My work habits throughout the writing process were_____

_____

_____

_____

My goals for improvement include _____

_____

_____

_____

Finding Your Topic

Objective: The students will brainstorm topics for descriptive writing, select one, and create an action plan for writing the description.

Procedure

1. Distribute "Finding Your Topic" (page 16). Lead a brainstorming session to help students complete the first question. Possible answers include: nature, animals, house, best friend, family member, school, the mall, etc.

2. Have students choose one of these topics and help them select something even more specific about the topic:

   For example, for nature one might choose a forest stream.

3. Discuss the creation of an action plan. Where do students need to go to read, listen, or view information regarding their topic? Do they need to visit a zoo or park? Read books? Look on the Internet? Ask them to list the steps they would need to take on the reproducible.

4. To connect descriptive writing to the content areas, have students brainstorm books or stories related to topics that they want to describe. For example, if students want to describe something particular in nature, have them use their science textbook as a reference. Have them evaluate the usefulness of their textbook in helping describe their topic.

Portfolio Piece: Have students put their brainstorming lists in their portfolios.

Publishing: Create a bulletin board of possible writing topics. Group the topics by category for easy selection.

Technology Connection: Have students use Internet search engines such as *Yahoo!* or *Excite* to research their topics for descriptive writing.

Home-School Connection: Have students brainstorm possible topics with a family member. Remind the students to look in their home libraries for ideas.

Assessment: Evaluate the students' ability to complete the "Finding Your Topic."

Finding Your Topic *(cont.)*

Directions: Complete the following worksheet in order to determine your topic for descriptive writing.

1. Brainstorm four possible topics of writing. Circle the one on which you will focus.
2. Choose something very specific within the topic.
3. Brainstorm and prioritize a list of action steps necessary to gather information on the topic.

Action Plan for Writing on the Topic	Prioritize the List
_____ _____	 _____
_____ _____	 _____
_____ _____	 _____
_____ _____	 _____

Focusing a Topic

Objective: The students will ask questions about a broad topic in order to narrow the topic and focus their writing.

Procedure

1. Read aloud the "Example of a Description of Setting" (page 10) and ask students to listen for the main idea or focus of the first paragraph.

2. On the board or overhead, identify the author's focus in the first paragraph. Then, identify subtopics from the paragraph that support and elaborate on the main focus.

3. Have students brainstorm a number of broad topics such as weather, careers, animals, transportation, etc.

4. With your guidance, have students answer the questions on the reproducible entitled, "Focusing a Topic" (page 18).

5. Have students work together in pairs and share their topic-focusing worksheets. Give students colored pencils to make revisions after they complete the worksheets.

6. Have students freewrite about the broad topic they have selected. Then, have them highlight words or phrases that strike them as interesting or unusual. Use these interesting words or phrases to focus the topic.

Portfolio Piece: Instruct students to use their focus worksheets to write a descriptive paragraph. Have students reread their writing and write a reflection about their strengths and weaknesses with regards to focusing their topics.

Publishing: Create more focus worksheets for students to complete and store in their portfolios for future use.

Technology Connection: Have students use their focus worksheets to write a descriptive email message to a friend about the topic. Have students ask their email buddy to answer the question, "What is the focus of this email message?"

Home School Connection: Instruct the students to use the focus questions during a dinner conversation to narrow the discussion.

Assessment: Assess the students' ability to accurately complete the "Focusing a Topic for Descriptive Writing" worksheet with sufficient detail.

Focusing a Topic *(cont.)*

Directions: Use the questions below to focus the topic of your descriptive writing.

Broad Topic: _____

1) What do I already know about this topic? List three or more things.

   _____

   _____

   _____

2) What do I want to learn about this topic? What questions do I have about this topic? List two questions.

   _____

   _____

   _____

3) Which question is intriguing to me? Why?

   _____

   _____

   _____

   _____

4) What resources do I have available to me in order to learn more about this topic?

   _____

   _____

   _____

5) Who can I interview about this topic?

   _____

   _____

   _____

6) Write a question that focuses your topic.

   _____

   _____

   _____

Using Graphic Organizers

Objective: The students will use graphic organizers to brainstorm ideas for descriptive writing.

Procedure

1. Introduce the students to six different kinds of graphic organizers that can help them plan their descriptive writing: Sensory Web (page 20), Character Chart (page 21), Setting Chart (page 22), Action Chart (page 23), Object Chart (page 24), and 5 Ws and How Organizer (page 25). Show students each of the graphic organizers and explain that many authors use different graphic organizers to plan their writing based on their purpose.

2. Read the "Example of a Description of Character" (page 11) and ask students to use the appropriate graphic organizer to take apart and analyze the author's writing.

3. With the students, brainstorm topics for their descriptive writing.

4. Have students conduct research or an observation of their topic and then use one of the graphic organizers to plan their writing.

Portfolio Piece: Instruct students to include their graphic organizers and rough drafts of descriptive writing in their portfolios as demonstration of the writing process. Have them write a reflection about the benefits of using a graphic organizer.

Publishing: 1) Create a bulletin board of the students' graphic organizers. 2) Share graphic organizers in partners and discuss the benefits of using them.

Technology Connection: Create original graphic organizers using the computer programs *Student Writing Center* or *Inspiration*.

Home-School Connection: Have students use a web with a family member to brainstorm attributes for an ideal summer vacation spot. Then research real vacation spots and compare their attributes to the brainstormed lists.

Assessment: Assess the students' ability to choose the appropriate graphic organizer to plan their descriptive writing.

Sensory Web

Directions: Use the following graphic organizer to brainstorm sensory details about the topic of your descriptive writing.

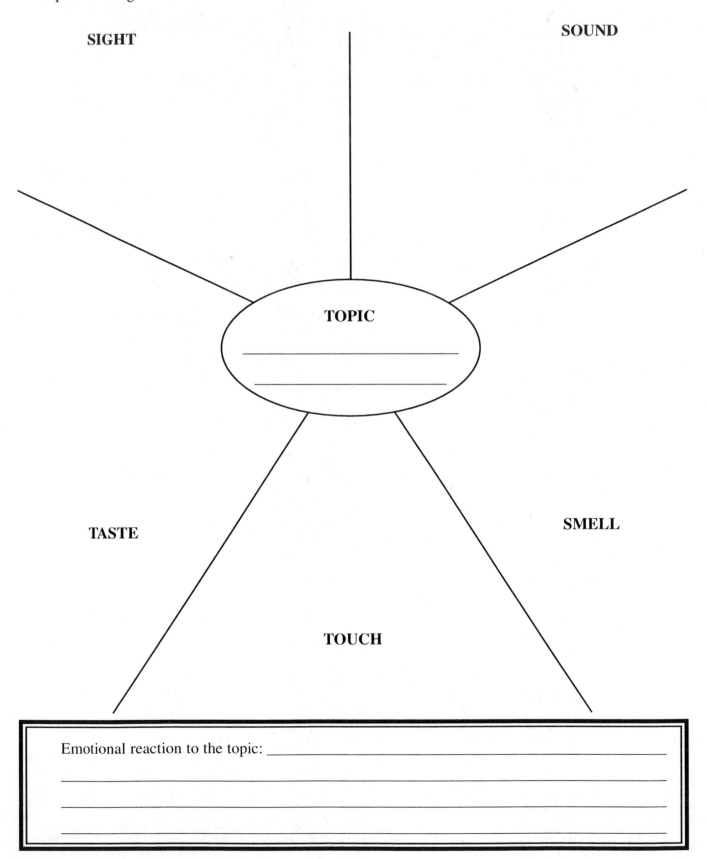

SIGHT

SOUND

TOPIC
_____
_____

TASTE

SMELL

TOUCH

Emotional reaction to the topic: _____
_____
_____
_____

Character Chart

Directions: Use the Character Chart below to record your observations of a real or fictional person in preparation of composing a piece of descriptive writing.

Character or Person's name: _____

Description of Face and Head (hair color/length, eye size and color, nose shape, head shape, mouth shape, size of ears, shape of eyebrows, length of eyelashes, bone structure, color and texture of complexion)	
Description of Body (height, weight, build, bone structure, size of feet and hands, color and texture of skin, body hair, and other unusual features)	
Description of Clothing (color and style, texture of fabric, shapes and patterns on fabric, tight vs. loose fit, pockets, embroidery, patches, trim, or other additions to the clothing, new vs. old, trendy vs. not trendy, bright vs. dull)	
Description of Accessories (earrings, necklace, bracelet, other jewelry, hat, belt, shoes, watch, coat, jacket, scarf, glasses, headband, barrette, and other hair accessories.)	
Description of Movement (graceful vs. awkward, body and facial gestures, confident vs. shy, posture, etc.)	
Description of Voice (high- or low-pitched, soft, smooth, raspy, shrill, husky, accent, etc.)	

Setting Chart

Directions: Use the following graphic organizer to record your observations of a setting in preparation for composing a descriptive piece of writing.

Word or phrase to identify setting: _____

Sights	Sounds	Tastes

Touches	Smells	Emotional Reaction

Action Chart

Directions: Use the following graphic organizer to gather ideas for writing descriptively about an action scene.

Setting of Action	Characters Involved	Source of Action or Conflict

Eventual Outcome of Conflict or Action	Vivid Verbs to Make Action Come Alive	Overall Desired Mood

Object Chart

Directions: Use the following graphic organizer to gather ideas for writing descriptively about a particular object.

Object: _____

Color, Texture, Size, and Shape of the Object	Sounds and Smells Associated with the Object	Usual Location of the Object

Uses and Purpose of the Object	Memory Associated with the Object	Unusual Features of the Object

5 Ws and How Organizer

Directions: Use the following graphic organizer to gather your ideas for your descriptive piece of writing.

Topic: _____

Who?	What?

Where?	When?

Why?	How?

Emotional Reaction to the Topic: _____

_____

_____

Observing the World Around You

Objective: The students will use observation techniques to gather information to compose a descriptive piece of writing.

Procedure

1. Define observation for the students on the chalkboard or overhead: *Observation involves reading, listening and/or watching carefully to learn all of the sensory detail necessary to accurately describe a location, person, or conflict. A graphic organizer can help record these details.*

2. Read a descriptive piece of writing to the students and have the students record the sensory details as well as their emotional response on the "Observation Guide" (page 27).

3. Next, divide students into pairs to share their "Observation Guides." Encourage students to get ideas from each other for making their worksheets more complete.

4. Have the students use the details to compose their own piece of descriptive writing.

Portfolio Piece: Instruct the students to include their "Observation Guides" in their portfolios. Have the students write a reflection in which they identify their greatest challenge when recording their observations about a particular subject.

Publishing: Publish the students' descriptive writing paragraphs about their surroundings in a classroom newspaper. Invite parents to a publication party.

Technology Connection: Have students research a particular subject on the Internet and use an "Observation Guide" to record the details conveyed by multimedia. Then have them use their completed guides to write a descriptive paragraph.

Home-School Connection: Instruct the students to watch a favorite TV show with a family member and take notes together on the "Observation Guide."

Assessment: Evaluate the students' ability to complete the "Observation Guide" with accuracy. Read the students' final descriptive writing and evaluate their ability to use observations in their descriptive writing.

Observation Guide

Directions: Choose a subject to observe and complete the following activities.

Subject being observed: _____   Date: _____

Time of day or night: _____

Purpose for observation: _____

Observe the subject carefully and record details that appeal to your senses in the chart below.

Sight	Sound	Smell	Touch	Taste

Emotional reaction to the subject: _____

Interviewing

Objective: The student will interview an expert on a topic for descriptive writing.

Procedure

1. Have students brainstorm and identify a writing topic for which it would be interesting to interview an expert. Then, have them brainstorm possible experts to interview.

2. Distribute and review "Interviewing" worksheet (page 29). Have the students brainstorm and write any questions they would like to ask the expert.

3. Inform students that good interviewers come to the interview prepared with questions; listen patiently for the interviewee to answer; take notes during the interview; and plan follow-up questions.

4. Students should arrange with their experts a time for an interview, during which they should take notes on their interview worksheets.

5. To connect this activity to science or social studies content, divide students into pairs and have one student take on the persona of an expert about a topic that is currently being studied. One student will play the role of an expert, while the other student interviews the "expert" student. Have each student prepare and study for his/her role.

Portfolio Piece: Have students write a reflection in which they identify the most effective question that they asked in the interview. Also, have students identify their strengths and weaknesses as interviewers.

Publishing: On a bulletin board, post students' "Interviewing" sheets alongside their descriptive writing, with the interview information highlighted.

Technology Connection: Have students conduct an online interview using a tool such as *Yahoo! Instant Messenger.*

Home-School Connection: Have students interview a family member about his/her job. Students should specifically practice their listening and note-taking skills in this exercise.

Assessment: Evaluate students' interview worksheets for completeness and evaluate the students' ability to incorporate the interview information into their descriptive writing.

Interviewing *(cont.)*

Directions: Use the following worksheet to interview an expert on the topic about which you will be writing your descriptive composition.

Topic: _____

1. What is your position?_____

2. What are some specific sensory details that can describe this topic?_____

_____

_____

3. How did you learn this information?_____

_____

_____

4. Could you show me an example or tell me a story to illustrate what you know about the topic?

_____

_____

_____

_____

5. What will my audience need to know about this topic? _____

_____

_____

_____

_____

6. Who else could I interview to find out more information about this topic?_____

_____

Audience in Descriptive Writing

Objective: The students will use knowledge of an audience to appeal to its emotions and interests when writing descriptively.

Procedure

1. Ask the students to brainstorm different groups of audiences, e.g., parents, firefighters, moviegoers, etc.

2. Read aloud the "Audience Analysis Guide for Descriptive Writing" (pages 31 and 32). Students can keep these questions in mind you read aloud the "Example of a Description of Character" (page 11), pausing throughout the reading to discuss the clues the author gives about knowledge of the audience.

3. Have students complete the "Audience Analysis Guide for Descriptive Writing" in response to the writing on page 11. Remind the students to make inferences based on their own lives since they are part of the intended audience.

4. Ask the students to find specific places in the text that show that the author is using his/her knowledge of the audience.

5. Have students select a topic for descriptive writing, then have them complete the "Audience Analysis Guide for Descriptive Writing" to anticipate the needs, dreams, hopes, and priorities of their intended audience.

Portfolio Piece: Pair students and have them listen to each other's descriptive writing. Then, have them discuss whether their partner's piece addressed an identified audience. Students can write a reflective letter about this process.

Publishing: Create a bulletin board and post the students' "Audience Analyses" along with illustrations of the audience.

Technology Connection: Have students read descriptive writing online and complete the "Audience Analysis Guide for Descriptive Writing."

Home-School Connection: Instruct students to discuss commercials on TV with a family member. Have students identify the assumptions the creators make about their audience.

Assessment: Evaluate students' ability to respond to each of the items listed on the analysis guide with accuracy and insight.

Audience Analysis Guide for Descriptive Writing

Directions: Respond to the following questions in order to get to know the audience. You can use this guide in two ways.

Option #1: Read a descriptive article, story, paragraph, or essay and complete the guide in order to understand the audience the author is trying to reach. You will have to make inferences using the author's vocabulary; sentence length; examples; and appeals to the audience's interests, dreams, or priorities. Since you are part of the audience, you can draw on your own life to answer the questions.

Option #2: To understand your own intended audience better, use this worksheet to guide you before you write a descriptive article, story, paragraph, or essay.

1. What is the age and gender of the intended audience? _____
   _____

2. What is the highest level of education of the audience? _____
   _____

3. What is the audience's type of work? _____ _____

4. Where does the audience live (city, rural, suburban, house, apartment, etc.)? _____
   _____

5. What are the audience's interests? _____
   _____

6. What kind of a setting does the audience appreciate? How do you know? _____
   _____

7. What kind of a person does the audience appreciate? How do you know? _____
   _____

8. Identify something that is very important to the audience. How do you know? _____
   _____
   _____
   _____

Audience Analysis Guide for
Descriptive Writing *(cont.)*

9. What concerns the audience? _____

_____

10. What makes the audience laugh? _____

_____

11. What gives the audience hope? _____

_____

12. What does the audience fear most? _____

_____

_____

_____

13. What might the audience already know about the topic? _____

_____

_____

_____

_____

14. What does the audience want to know about the topic? _____

_____

_____

Leads

Objective: The students will write a lead that develops the reader's interest and introduces the descriptive writing topic.

Procedure

1. Write a definition of a *lead* on the chalkboard or overhead: *A lead is the way the author starts the text. Leads must "grab" the reader and entice him/her to read on.*

2. Read aloud the "Example of a Description of Action" (page 12). Discuss with the students the following questions: Does this lead grab your attention? Why or why not? What words or phrases help develop your interest? What is the topic of this descriptive piece of writing?

3. Display the reproducible entitled, "Kinds of Leads for Descriptive Writing" (page 34).

4. Have the students brainstorm a topic. Instruct them to write two different leads for this topic and use the reproducible to guide their drafting.

5. Divide the students into pairs and have them read each of their leads aloud to their partners. Have partners choose the lead that is the most engaging.

Portfolio Piece: Have students write leads to be included in their portfolios. Ask students to also write a reflection explaining how the kind of lead they chose will grab their reader's interest and make him/her want to read further.

Publishing: Create an interactive bulletin board with student samples of each kind of lead posted on the board. Make a folder of sentence strips identifying each kind of lead. Students can match the kind of lead with the student example.

Technology Connection: Have students use a word-processing program to write their leads. Encourage students to use spell check and grammar check.

Home-School Connection: Have students read a descriptive piece of writing in a magazine, highlight the lead, and discuss the method used to write the lead with a family member.

Assessment: Use the rubric for descriptive writing on page 14 to score the students' leads.

Kinds of Leads for Descriptive Writing

Strong leads engage the reader. Read the examples below to learn how to get the reader's attention.

Lead #1: Use strong visual imagery

Red, orange, gold, and yellow—such are the colors of a glorious autumn day.

Lead #2: Use dialogue

"Christina, it might be wise to wear a light sweater today." As mom and daughter prepared to go outside, they discussed their plans for the day. As they stepped foot outside, they felt the chill in the air as the red, gold, and orange leaves drifted to the ground. A squirrel played behind the magnolia tree as Christina and her mother climbed into their dark blue sedan.

Lead #3: Use repetition of verbs

Imagine a gorgeous autumn day where the trees are turning yellow, orange, and red. Imagine the squirrels gathering nuts and acorns preparing for winter. Imagine the slight chill in the air as the days get longer and longer. Imagine the sound of the crunching leaves as you walk along the blanket of dead leaves covering the yards and sidewalks.

Lead #4: Use a personal story

I remember the time that I traveled to my grandmother's house for her autumn birthday. My mom, dad, sister, and I made the six-hour journey in our minivan reading stories and singing songs along the way. As we traveled up the East Coast, we went through Maryland, Pennsylvania, New York, Connecticut, and Massachusetts. As we approached each state, I made a prediction about the status of the trees. The further north we went, the more vibrant colors we encountered. Reds, oranges, golds, and yellows filled the landscaping, reminding us of the glorious celebration of the seasons.

Lead #5: Use a rhetorical question

Have you ever gone outside on an autumn day and been overwhelmed by the explosion of orange, red, gold, and yellow in front of you?

Lead #6: Use a simile or metaphor

The red, orange, gold, and yellow leaves filled the horizon with brilliant color. As we traveled along the road, the vibrant trees looked like huge bouquets gathered for a special occasion.

Using Supporting Details

Objective: The student will write a lead, subtopics, and supporting details for a descriptive writing topic.

Procedure

1. Present the students with the topic of a summer day. Have the students create a lead for this topic by referring to "Kinds of Leads for Descriptive Writing" (page 34).

2. Discuss and brainstorm with the students what they need to do to find supporting details for their topic of a summer day.

3. Instruct the students to think of their own topics. Students may want to use "Finding Your Topic" (page 16).

4. Have students complete "Using Supporting Details" (page 36). Guide students when writing their topic sentences and supporting details. You may want to model how to use the reproducible on the overhead. For example:

   Subtopic: Heat

   Supporting Details: sweltering, muggy, causes people to want to go swimming, hazy, sweating, drinking cold drinks, etc.

5. Have the students use the "Observation Guide" (page 27) or the "Interviewing" worksheet (page 29) to gather more information about their topic if necessary.

Portfolio Piece: Have students use their "Using Supporting Details" worksheets as the basis for a descriptive piece of writing and write a reflection about the process.

Publishing: Have the students illustrate their descriptive pieces of writing and publish the writing in a class anthology of descriptive writing.

Technology Connection: Use a digital camera to take pictures of the students' topics. Post pictures and descriptive writing in the school showcase.

Home-School Connection: Instruct students to interview their parents about their topic to gather more details.

Assessment: 1. Evaluate the students' descriptive writing specifically for the skill of providing adequate supporting detail. 2. Assess the completion and accuracy of the reproducible entitled "Using Supporting Details."

Using Supporting Details *(cont.)*

Directions: Identify your topic and write your lead in the space provided below. Then, brainstorm subtopics and supporting details. Supporting details may include descriptive adjectives, phrases, vivid verbs, and specific nouns that you associate with each subtopic.

Topic: _____

Lead:

_____

_____

_____

_____

_____

Subtopic: _____

Supporting Details: _____

_____

_____

Subtopic: _____

Supporting Details: _____

_____

_____

Subtopic: _____

Supporting Details: _____

_____

_____

Organizing Your Details

Objective: Students will identify a central theme or topic for their writing, brainstorm supporting details, and organize those details in order to give their writing appeal to the reader.

Procedure

1. Have students identify several topics about which they could compose a persuasive piece of writing.

2. Distribute "Organizing Your Details" (page 38). Instruct the students to choose one topic, identify a central theme for writing, and list at least three supporting details.

3. Use a student example to demonstrate how to organize supporting details. Inform the students that there are two ways to organize their points: ascending and descending. Ascending order means that the most important detail is last, and descending order means that the most important detail is first. Discuss the strengths and weaknesses of each approach.

4. Have the students rank order their supporting details on their worksheets. Have students share responses with a partner and gather feedback from peers on the strengths and weaknesses of their approach.

Portfolio Piece: Have students include their descriptive writing in their portfolios and write a reflection explaining how they decided to organize their supporting details.

Publishing: Create a bulletin board of the students' descriptive writing and post next to their writing the students' explanations for how they organized their supporting details.

Technology Connection: Have students use the cut and paste functions of a word-processing program to organize their supporting details in different ways.

Home-School Connection: Have students discuss with a family member three details about their house. Have them organize these details in a way that is most appealing to their audience. Students will share their organized details in class.

Assessment: Use the rubric for descriptive writing on page 14 and evaluate the students' abilities to organize their supporting details to be most appealing to the audience.

Organizing Your Details *(cont.)*

Directions: Use this worksheet to organize the details of your descriptive writing.

Topic: _____   **Audience:** _____

Purpose: _____

_____

Theme: _____

_____

Supporting Details for Your Theme	Order
_____ _____	_____
_____ _____	_____
_____ _____	_____
_____ _____	_____
_____ _____	_____
_____ _____	_____

Linking Details Using Transitions

Objective: The students will use transitions to link details in descriptive writing.

Procedure

1. Inform the students that they need to link the ideas between and within their paragraphs by using transitions. Write the following transition words and phrases on the board: *first, second, third, next, additionally, in addition, also, last, finally, for example, similarly, by contrast.*

2. Have students use their "Organizing Your Details" worksheet (page 38) to complete "Linking Details Using Transitions" (page 40). Have students put their supporting details in order and choose an appropriate transition to link each supporting detail to the next detail.

3. Instruct students to draft their descriptive writing using the transition worksheet.

4. When the students are finished drafting their worksheets, have them highlight each of the transitions that they used. If they can't highlight any transitions, have them go back and add appropriate transitions.

5. Divide the students into pairs and have them read their drafts aloud to each other, paying attention to whether or not the transitions help the flow of the piece.

Portfolio Piece: Have students include their descriptive writing in their portfolios with the transitions highlighted.

Publishing: Create a bulletin board of the students' descriptive writing with the transitions highlighted. Scatter sentence strips printed with transitions around the writing.

Technology Connection: Have students use the thesaurus function to come up with alternative transition words and phrases.

Home-School Connection: Have students read several pieces of descriptive writing with a family member and create a word bank of transitions that are effective. Instruct the students to post the list next to their desk at home as a reference.

Assessment: 1. Evaluate the students' ability to complete the worksheet "Linking Details Using Transitions." 2. Read the students' descriptive writing and evaluate their appropriate use of transitions within their writing.

Linking Details Using Transitions *(cont.)*

Directions: Use the following activity to link your details together by using transitions. Read the transitions for linking details, identify each of your details in the worksheet below, and select an appropriate transition to connect each detail.

Commonly used transitions for linking details include *first, second, third, next, additionally, in addition, also, last, finally, for example, similarly, by contrast, however, therefore, finally.*

Transition: _____

Detail #1: _____

_____

_____

Transition: _____

Detail #2: _____

_____

_____

Transition: _____

Detail #3: _____

_____

_____

Transition: _____

Detail #4: _____

_____

_____

Writing Conclusions

Objective: The students will write conclusions that connect, summarize, and extend the ideas presented in the body of their work.

Procedure

1. Present the criteria of a conclusion to the students as listed on "Writing Conclusions" (page 42).

2. Have students underline information related to the main theme of a piece of writing and circle any main ideas that connect to the theme. Then have them write rough drafts of their conclusions using "Writing Conclusions."

3. Pair the students and have them read each other's conclusions and check them against the criteria for a conclusion listed at the top of "Writing Conclusions." Have students redraft their conclusions using their partner's suggestions.

4. Have students switch papers and write alternative conclusions to each other's descriptive writing. Have them compare and contrast and decide which conclusion is more effective using the criteria for a conclusion.

Portfolio Piece: Have the students write two different conclusions for their writing. Then, have them select the best one and write a reflection letter in which they identify how they used the conclusion criteria to select the best conclusion.

Publishing: Have students read their conclusions out loud to the class. Instruct the student audience to identify the main theme and the supporting details of a student's piece based on the information in the conclusion.

Technology Connection: Have students use a word-processing program to cut and paste information related to the main theme and supporting details. Then have them create a logical conclusion.

Home-School Connection: Instruct students to have a dinner conversation about a particular topic appropriate for descriptive writing. Have the students identify the main theme connected to their topic with a family member.

Assessment: Use the rubric for descriptive writing on page 14 to score the student's conclusion. Allow each student to self-evaluate by completing the "self" portion of the rubric. Allow students to work with peers and complete the "peer" portion of the rubric. Students can make revisions after this process.

Writing Conclusions *(cont.)*

Directions: Use this worksheet to write a complete conclusion that extends your main ideas. Good conclusions:

- begin with a summary statement
- connect the main ideas presented in the body of your descriptive writing
- connect back to themes presented in the introduction
- connect the ideas in the summary to personal experiences or events and ideas beyond the text.

Use information from the introduction and body of your descriptive writing to complete the following:

Central theme or idea: _____

Two or three supporting ideas from your descriptive writing: _____

_____

_____

_____

Now write a conclusion for this piece of descriptive writing:

Your summary statement: _____

A sentence or two connecting to the ideas or details woven throughout your writing: _____

_____

_____

_____

A sentence that connects the main ideas to other information "beyond the text": _____

_____

_____

Voice

Objective: The student will identify an author's voice in a descriptive piece of writing and then find their own authorial voices.

Procedure

1. Write a definition of voice on the board: *Voice is the way the author talks about a subject that reveals his/her personality, as well as his/her feelings about the subject.*

2. On the board or overhead, brainstorm a list of more words that would be helpful in identifying the voice of the author, such as friendly, sarcastic, appreciative, skeptical, reserved, enthusiastic, overwhelmed, surprised, etc.

3. Read "Example of a Description of Action" (page 12) and ask students to listen for the author's voice. When you have finished reading, discuss with the students which words or sentences describe the voice of the writer. Use "Identifying Voice" (page 44) to record the students' responses.

4. Have students write about a recent school event. When they are finished, have them highlight or underline words that reveal their feelings about the topic.

Portfolio Piece: Instruct students to compose a descriptive piece of writing about some aspect of school. Then, have the students highlight or underline all of the words or sentences that reveal their beliefs on the topic.

Publishing: Create a bulletin board of the students' descriptive writing. On colorful construction paper, have the students write a single word that reveals their feelings about the topic that they wrote about in their descriptive writing.

Technology Connection: Have students write email messages to online buddies about a topic they are learning about in science or social studies class that conveys their feeling, or voice, about that topic.

Home-School Connection: Have students read descriptive pieces of writing from magazines and discuss with their parents the effect that voice has upon the reader.

Assessment: Evaluate the students' understanding of voice by assessing the completeness and accuracy of the worksheet entitled "Identifying Voice."

Identifying Voice

Directions: Use the following graphic organizer to analyze the author's voice. You may also use this graphic organizer to analyze your own writing. Remember, voice is the way the author writes about a subject that reveals his/her personality, as well as his/her feelings about the topic.

Topic: _____   **Audience:** _____

Purpose: _____

_____

Theme: _____

_____

Words, Sentences, or Passages from Descriptive Writing	Author's Feelings or Beliefs about the Topic
_____	_____
_____	_____
_____	_____
_____	_____
_____	_____
_____	_____
_____	_____
_____	_____
_____	_____
_____	_____
_____	_____
_____	_____
_____	_____
_____	_____

Tone

Objectives: The students will identify the tone used in descriptive writing and apply the knowledge of tone to their own descriptive writing.

Procedure

1. Write a definition of *tone* on the board or overhead: *In descriptive writing, the tone of the writer should reflect his/her feelings about the subject.*

2. Instruct the students to use "Evaluating Tone" (page 46) to identify the subject, purpose, and audience of their writing. Brainstorm with the students their possible feelings about their subjects (excitement, anxiety, joy, confusion, etc.).

3. Have students record examples of words, phrases, or sentences from their own writing and then identify the feelings that the reader can infer from the writing.

4. Instruct the students to match the feelings that they determined from the actual text examples with their initial and intended feelings on the subject.

5. Have students read descriptive writing from magazines and other literature anthologies and identify the feelings of the author toward the subject.

Portfolio Piece: Instruct students to compose a descriptive piece of writing and highlight places in the letter where the tone of the writer is demonstrated. Have them write a reflection on how the tone of their writing might affect an audience.

Publishing: Have the students give a piece of their writing to an audience with a request that the audience identifies the author's feelings toward the subject. Did the student author do his or her job?

Technology Connection: Have students read descriptive writing online and identify the tone of the author.

Home-School Connection: Have students discuss with a family member the tone of a particular descriptive piece of writing.

Assessment: Evaluate the students' ability to adequately complete "Evaluating Tone."

Evaluating Tone

Directions: Use this worksheet to examine the tone in your descriptive writing.

Subject: _____

Purpose for writing: _____

Audience: _____

Feelings about the subject: _____

Example from your writing (key words, phrases, sentences from the text)	What do these examples from the text reveal in terms of your feelings about the subject?
_____ _____ _____ _____ _____	_____ _____ _____ _____ _____
_____ _____ _____ _____ _____	_____ _____ _____ _____ _____
_____ _____ _____ _____ _____	_____ _____ _____ _____ _____

Mood

Objective: The students will listen to a peer's descriptive writing draft and identify how the subject of the piece of writing influenced their feelings and thoughts.

Procedure

1. Show the students a series of drawn faces that each show a different expression that reveals an emotion. Discuss the affect or mood that is shown by each.

2. Inform the students that *mood is the feeling that the audience has after reading the work of a particular author, listening to a song, or watching a movie.*

3. Have students listen to a story or song that has descriptive imagery; then lead a discussion about how the subject influenced the students' feelings and thoughts. Have students choose specific words, phrases, or sentences from the story or song that helped to influence their feelings. Use "Identifying Mood" (page 48) to guide your discussion.

4. Pair the students and have them read aloud the rough drafts of their descriptive pieces of writing and identify the mood (if any) that they feel as a result of listening to their partner's drafts.

Portfolio Piece: Have students include their paragraphs in their portfolios and write a reflection on the importance of connecting with the thoughts and feelings of the audience.

Publishing: Have students write descriptions of a favorite vacation spot. Then have them share their descriptions with small groups and identify the mood of the authors of the descriptive writing.

Technology Connection: E-mail a friend about a recent day in school. After describing the day at school, instruct students to ask their email buddies to describe their feelings about the subject. If the student did a good job on the description, the buddies should be able to easily identify their feelings on the subject.

Home-School Connection: Have students look through magazines with a family member and focus on their mood when viewing the advertisements.

Assessment: Evaluate the students' understanding of mood by checking the "Identifying Mood" worksheet for completeness.

Identifying Mood

Directions: Use this worksheet to identify a writer's feelings on a subject. Select at least three key sentences and identify your resulting feelings on the subject.

Title: _____

Purpose of Writing: _____

Audience: _____

Key Sentences from the Descriptive Piece of Writing	Your Resulting Feelings and Thoughts

Do you think your mood that resulted from reading or listening to the descriptive piece of writing was what the author intended you to feel? Why or why not?

_____

_____

_____

_____

Identifying Theme

Objective: The students will identify a theme in published descriptive writing and incorporate a theme into their own descriptive writing.

Procedure

1. Write a definition of theme on the chalkboard: *A theme is the central message or key idea that the writer wants to convey to the reader. Often, the reader has to infer the theme by thinking carefully about the events, conflicts, or images in the piece of writing and the writer's main purpose.*

2. Read "Example of a Description of Action" (page 12) and have the students identify the theme in the writing.

3. Have the students brainstorm topics for their descriptive writing and write rough drafts. Students can highlight any conflict or key images that reveal theme.

4. Review and assign "Theme in Descriptive Writing" (page 50).

5. Have the students reread their draft with the purpose of strengthening their theme.

6. Pair students. Have them share their drafts and discuss the following question: What needs to be added, changed, or deleted to improve the theme? Allow students time to make revisions to their drafts based on their peer's feedback.

Portfolio Piece: Have the students write a reflection in which they identify the greatest challenge that they faced when incorporating theme into their descriptive writing.

Publishing: Post the students' writing on a bulletin board along with several themes written on colorful paper.

Technology Connection: Have the students use a word-processing program to make revisions to their descriptive writing.

Home-School Connection: Have the students discuss themes with their family members, choose a favorite theme, and articulate why this theme is compelling.

Assessment:

1. Assess the students' ability to complete the reproducible entitled "Theme in Descriptive Writing."

2. Evaluate students' descriptive writing for the effective use of theme.

Theme in Descriptive Writing

Directions: Read the following information carefully and then complete the activities at the bottom of the page. You may use this worksheet to analyze your own or someone else's descriptive writing.

Definition: A theme is the central message or key idea that the writer wants to convey to the reader. Often, the reader has to infer the theme by thinking carefully about the events, conflicts, or images in the piece of writing and the writer's main purpose.

Possible themes:

- Love conquers all.
- Human spirit triumphs over strife.
- Animals provide great comfort to humans.
- Relationships are important to the fulfillment of the human spirit.
- Hard work pays off.
- Nature calms the human spirit.
- Humans are in awe of nature.

Conflict:

_____

_____

_____

Outcome of Conflict:

_____

_____

_____

Key Images from Text:

_____

_____

_____

Central Theme: (Message that the writer wants to convey to the reader)

_____

_____

_____

Describing Conflict

Objective: The students will write brief descriptions of conflict.

Procedure

1. Ask the students to define the word conflict. Possible responses include problems, obstacles, hurdles, anger, fighting, and sadness. Inform the students that often descriptive writing has an underlying element of conflict.

2. Instruct the students to read a descriptive piece of writing that includes some conflict. Then, have the students complete "Describing Conflict" (page 52), referring to the text in order to answer the questions with supporting details.

3. Have the students share their responses with a partner and make sure that their answers are complete and detailed.

4. Have the students use the worksheet "Describing Conflict" to identify a conflict and compose a descriptive piece of writing that incorporates an intriguing and meaningful conflict.

Portfolio Piece: Have the students write a reflection identifying their greatest challenge when incorporating conflict into a descriptive piece of writing.

Publishing: In round-robin fashion, have the students share the conflict they will incorporate into their descriptive pieces of writing. On the chalkboard or overhead, record the students' responses. Then, have students elaborate on and add to the list of conflicts that have been generated on the chalkboard.

Technology Connection: Have students use a word-processing program to compose their descriptive writing and then choose an appropriate graphic to represent the conflict they have incorporated into their writing. Have students create a text box and use the wrapping function in order to integrate the graphic into the text.

Home-School Connection: Have the students discuss the following questions with a family member: What conflicts do I face at school? What conflicts do I face at home? How do I overcome these conflicts?

Assessment: Evaluate the students' "Describing Conflict" worksheets for completeness and accuracy.

Describing Conflict *(cont.)*

Directions: In the space provided below, identify the conflict to be incorporated into your descriptive piece of writing. Then, in the boxes, write some words and phrases that will help you to reveal the conflict to the reader.

Subject: _____

Purpose: _____

Conflict: _____

Images that will reveal conflict	Adjectives that will reveal conflict
_____ _____ _____ _____	_____ _____ _____ _____

Vivid verbs that will reveal conflict	Similes and/or metaphors that will reveal conflict
_____ _____ _____ _____	_____ _____ _____ _____

The desired emotional response from the audience is _____

_____

_____

Building Style in Descriptive Writing

Objective: The students will write a paragraph using several elements of style in order to appeal to the audience.

Procedure

1. Write the following elements of style on the chalkboard: rhetorical questions, "imagine that . . ." sentence beginnings, imagery, adjectives, similes, and metaphors. Tell the students that using these elements of style will make their writing more interesting and appealing to the audience.

2. Read aloud the "Style in Descriptive Writing" reproducible (page 54) to the students. Give the students examples so that they understand each of the elements.

3. Read "Example of a Description of Setting" (page 10) and then complete the reproducible. As you read, record elements of style on the chart. Discuss with the students the effects that the elements of style have on their emotions and feelings about the topic of discussion.

4. Have students choose three of the elements of style and write a paragraph using the selected elements.

5. Divide students into pairs and have the students read each other's paragraphs. Have them use the "Peer Response to Style" worksheet (page 55) to give each other feedback.

Portfolio Piece: Have students include three elements of style in their descriptive writing and write a reflection in which they identify the ease or difficulty with which they were able to incorporate the elements of style.

Publishing: Pair students with children at another grade level. Have students share their best original stylistic element with their partner and ask for feedback.

Technology Connection: Have students use a word-processing program to revise their paragraphs by adding and deleting elements of style as necessary.

Home-School Connection: Have students brainstorm how many different elements of style they can use to describe a family meal.

Assessment: Evaluate the students' understanding of elements of style by reading and assessing their accurate completion of the "Peer Response to Style" worksheet.

Style in Descriptive Writing

Directions: Read the chart below that contains some elements of style. As you read, think about which elements of style you have included in your own writing.

Some Elements of Style	Definition and Reason for Use
Rhetorical question	The author asks a question to get the reader thinking about personal experiences related to the topic and questions/thoughts that the reader has about the topic. "Rhetorical" means that the author doesn't really expect the reader to answer the question.
"Imagine that . . ." sentence beginning	The author uses an "imagine that . . ." sentence beginning to spark the reader's imagination with images and thoughts related to the topic. Often the writer also uses sensory details within the "imagine that . . ." scenario to connect with the reader's thoughts and ideas.
Imagery	The author uses words and phrases to appeal to the reader's five senses. The author uses imagery to appeal to the readers' imaginations and help them create pictures in their minds.
Adjectives	The author uses adjectives to clarify nouns. A particularly powerful stylistic tool is to use three adjectives in a row for repetitive emphasis.
Similes	Similes use *like* or *as* to make a comparison. The author uses similes to create interesting pictures in the reader's mind.
Metaphors	Metaphors make a direct comparison and do not use *like* or *as*. The author uses metaphors to compare abstract concepts to concrete images so that the concept can be better understood.

Peer Response to Style

Writer's name: _____

Peer's name: _____

Directions:

Writers: Share your descriptive paragraph with your partner. Read slowly, so your peer can take notes about your stylistic elements. After you are finished reading, take notes about what your peer has observed about your writing.

Peers: Share your identification of stylistic elements with your partner and provide a rating for your peer. Share your observations slowly, so that the writer has time to take notes on the worksheet.

✔+ = Great!	✔ = Ok	✔– = Poor

Element of Style	Example from Text	Rating
_____ _____	_____ _____ _____ _____	_____
_____ _____	_____ _____ _____ _____	_____
_____ _____	_____ _____ _____ _____	_____

Varying Sentence Structure and Length

Objective: The students will vary sentence structure and length in descriptive writing in order to improve their understanding of style.

Procedure

1. Discuss the fact that there are three basic sentence structures: simple, compound, and complex. Authors vary their sentence structure in order to make their writing flow. Sentence length is the amount of words in the sentence. Authors vary their sentence length in order to create emphasis.

2. Have the students read a descriptive article in a magazine. Instruct them to count and record the sentence lengths of the first five sentences. Ask the students, "Are any of the sentences the same length?" and "Why wouldn't the author simply make all of the sentences the same?"

3. Give the students a simple topic (e.g., school, a park, an animal, a family member). Have the students choose one of these topics and brainstorm sensory details.

4. Have the students use the details to write a paragraph about their topic. Then, have the students reread and edit their work to vary the sentence structure and length.

5. Assign and discuss "Varying Sentence Structure and Length" (page 57).

Portfolio Piece: Have students include their sensory paragraphs in their portfolios. Have them identify the length and structure of their favorite sentence and explain why they think this sentence will impress an audience.

Publishing: Instruct the students to write a complex sentence about nature. Students can share their sentences with the class.

Technology Connection: Show students how to use the grammar-check function in a word-processing program to ensure they have avoided sentence fragments and run-ons.

Home-School Connection: Have the students read a short story with a family member and identify the sentence lengths of each of the sentences in the first paragraph.

Assessment: Evaluate the students' accurate completion of "Varying Sentence Structure and Length." Read the students' descriptive writing and determine if they have applied their knowledge of sentences to their writing.

Varying Sentence Structure
and Length *(cont.)*

Directions: Read the text of a descriptive piece of writing carefully and choose three sentences. Copy each of the sentences onto the chart and identify the word length and structure for each sentence. Then, as a class discuss the effectiveness of each of the sentences.

Varying Sentence Structure

Authors vary sentence structure to make their writing flow. By using a combination of simple, compound, and complex sentence structures, the mind of the reader more easily follows the arguments of the author.

Varying Sentence Length

Authors vary sentence length to create emphasis. Authors mostly use average and long sentences, but a short sentence every once in a while creates impact and is powerful to the reader.

Sentence	Word Length	Structure

Elaborating Using Prepositional Phrases

Objective: The students will use prepositional phrases to elaborate key points and supporting details in descriptive writing.

Procedure

1. Ask students to define what it means to elaborate and extend ideas in writing. Ask students to identify ways to extend writing such as using sensory details; adding adjectives, similes, and metaphors; inserting vivid verbs; and adding prepositional phrases.

2. Distribute "Elaborating Using Prepositional Phrases" (page 59). Review with the students the definition of a preposition and examples of prepositions.

3. Have the students complete the "Writer's Practice" section of the worksheet.

4. Instruct the students to reread the descriptive writing they have composed and highlight any prepositional phrases they have already included.

5. Have the students use colored pencils to add more prepositional phrases to extend ideas as appropriate. Model for the students how to do this by making a transparency of one of the students' pieces of descriptive writing and adding prepositional phrases as needed for the students to see on the overhead projector.

Portfolio Piece: Have the students write a reflection in which they identify whether or not the ideas in their descriptive writing are elaborate enough to meet the needs of the audience.

Publishing: Have the students create a prepositional poem. Give them a statement such as "The mouse ran. . . ." The students can then add four prepositional phrases.

Technology Connection: Have the students use a word-processing program to compose their descriptive writing and revise by adding prepositional phrases as needed.

Home-School Connection: Instruct the students to describe a recent event to a family member by using at least five prepositional phrases.

Assessment: Evaluate the students' ability to complete the 12 exercises in the "Writer's Practice" section of the reproducible accurately. In addition, assess the students' descriptive writing for appropriate use of prepositional phrases.

Elaborating Using Prepositional Phrases *(cont.)*

Directions: Read the information below and then complete the section entitled "Writer's Practice." Remember that a preposition is a word that shows the relationship between a noun, pronoun, or another word in a sentence.

Frequently Used Prepositions:

About	Behind	Except	Of	To
Across	Beneath	For	On	With
At	Between	From	Onto	Without
Around	Down	In	Over	Within
Before	During	Into	Through	Under

Writer's Practice: Circle the prepositional phrase in each sentence. Then write the preposition on the line next to the sentence.

1. The toad sat under the brown bench. _____

2. The little girl nestled between her parents. _____

3. Around the bend, a car was quickly approaching. _____

4. The ball landed behind the tall tree. _____

5. During the storm, a telephone pole fell. _____

6. After dinner, do your homework. _____

7. You got a postcard from dear Aunt Sally today. _____

8. Beneath the crevice hid a tiny squirrel. _____

9. The boy jumped onto the boat. _____

10. I will meet you at the restaurant tomorrow morning. _____

11. I finished all of my ice cream. _____

12. The little bunny scurried across the road. _____

Simile and Metaphor

Objective: The students will use similes and/or metaphors to create a picture in the reader's mind of the images, objects, and ideas being described.

Procedure

1. Write the following definitions of simile and metaphor on the chalkboard: *A simile uses like or as to compare one thing to another.* Example: Reading is *like* riding a roller coaster: full of ups and downs, times when you understand and times when you don't. A metaphor is a direct comparison that does not use like or as. Example: Reading is a roller coaster: full of ups and downs.

2. Read "Example of a Description of Setting" (page 10) and have the students identify the simile in the writing.

3. Have the students brainstorm topics for their descriptive writing and write rough drafts. Instruct the students to highlight places where they think similes and metaphors would be particularly effective.

4. Have the students choose two of the places they highlighted and add a simile and a metaphor.

5. Divide the students into partners and have the students share the similes and metaphors that they have added with their partner.

6. Allow students time to make revisions to their drafts based on their peer's feedback.

Portfolio Piece: Have the students write a reflection in which they identify how their writing is enhanced by the addition of similes and metaphors.

Publishing: Have the students write similes and metaphors about reading, writing, creating, and thinking. Post the similes and metaphors in the hallways and the classroom.

Technology Connection: Have the students use a word-processing program to make revisions to their descriptive writing.

Home-School Connection: Instruct the students to identify five household objects and describe these objects using either similes or metaphors.

Assessment: Evaluate students' descriptive writing for the effective use of similes and metaphors.

Alliteration and Assonance

Objective: The students will use alliteration and/or assonance to create emphasis in descriptive writing.

Procedure

1. Write the following definitions of alliteration and assonance on the chalkboard: *Alliteration is the repetition of consonant sounds at the beginnings of words. Assonance is the repetition of vowel sounds. Both alliteration and assonance are used to create rhythm and emphasis in writing.*

2. Read "Example of a Description of Action" (page 12) and have the students identify the alliteration and assonance in the writing. Ask the students to identify other places in the text where alliteration and/or assonance would be effective.

3. Have the students brainstorm topics for their descriptive writing and write rough drafts. If they already have drafts, have them place their drafts in front of them.

4. Instruct the students to go through their rough drafts and highlight places where they think that alliteration or assonance would be particularly effective.

5. Have the students complete the reproducible "Alliteration and Assonance" (page 62).

6. Divide the students into partners and have them share and discuss the alliteration and assonance that they have added.

7. Allow students time to make revisions to their drafts based on their peer's feedback.

Portfolio Piece: Have the students write a reflection in which they identify how their writing is enhanced by the addition of alliteration and assonance.

Publishing: Have the students share their writing in a round-robin fashion and praise the use of alliteration and assonance.

Technology Connection: Have the students use a word-processing program to make revisions to their descriptive writing.

Home-School Connection: Have the students share their rough drafts with a family member for feedback.

Assessment:

1. Assess the students' ability to complete "Alliteration and Assonance."

2. Evaluate students' descriptive writing for the effective use of alliteration and assonance.

Alliteration and Assonance *(cont.)*

Directions: Read the information below and complete each of the activities.

Definition:

Alliteration is the repetition of consonant sounds at the beginnings of words. Assonance is the repetition of vowel sounds. Both alliteration and assonance are used to create rhythm and emphasis in writing.

Writer's Practice:

Identify the alliteration or assonance in each of the following sentences by underlining the consonants or vowels that are being repeated. In the space provided, identify whether the technique in each sentence is alliteration or assonance.

1. The climbing clematis vine encircled the lamp post. _____

2. The stone cold soldier rowed the boat to the nearby shore. _____

3. It was a misty Monday as the motorists meandered down the highway. _____

4. Fame came easily to the dame who wore the magnificent gold chain. _____

Adding to Your Draft

Reread your rough draft and identify three places that you could add alliteration and/or assonance. Complete the activity below.

Paragraph of Your Draft	Existing Word or Phrase	Phrase with Added Alliteration or Assonance

Repetition

Objective: The students will use repetition in descriptive writing in order to create emphasis.

Procedure

1. Write a definition of repetition on the chalkboard: *Repetition is the use of sentences, phrases, words, parts of words, or sounds more than once in order to create emphasis.*

2. Read "Example of a Description of Setting" (page 10) and have the students identify the repetition in the writing.

3. Have the students brainstorm topics for their descriptive writing and write rough drafts.

4. Review "Using Repetition" (page 64) with the students. Pay attention to all the different ways to use repetition. Then direct students to go through their drafts as instructed on the worksheet.

5. Have the students add repetition to their drafts. Circulate around the room, offering guidance as needed. As the students are working, have some of the students who have done a good job adding repetition share their examples.

7. Divide the students into partners and have the students share the repetition that they have added with their partner.

8. Allow students time to revise their drafts based on their peer's feedback.

Portfolio Piece: Have the students write a reflection in which they identify the greatest challenge that they faced when adding repetition to their descriptive writing.

Publishing: Post the students' writing on a bulletin board. Have the students highlight their use of repetition.

Technology Connection: Have the students use a word-processing program to revise their descriptive writing.

Home-School Connection: Have the students identify with their family members several favorite songs. Instruct the students to listen to one of the songs and identify any repetition and why the songwriter chose to include repetition.

Assessment:

1. Assess the students' ability to complete the reproducible entitled "Using Repetition."

2. Evaluate students' descriptive writing for the effective use of repetition.

Using Repetition

Directions: Read the information below and complete the activity at the bottom of the page.

Definition

Repetition is the use of sentences, phrases, words, parts of words, or sounds more than once in order to create emphasis.

Some Forms of Repetition:

- Repetition of a word prefix or suffix
- Repetition of a particular part of speech (nouns, adjectives, verbs, interjections, prepositions, conjunctions)
- Repetition of infinitives, participles, or gerunds
- Repetition of a single word (consecutively repeated or sprinkled throughout the text)
- Repetition of a phrase
- Repetition of a sentence structure

Adding to Your Draft

Reread your draft and notice all the places that you highlighted as possibilities for adding repetition. Brainstorm repetition possibilities in the spaces provided below. When you are finished, check (✔) your three best examples in the right hand column.

Page and Paragraph of Your Draft	Repetition to be Added	Check if you have decided to add the repetition to your draft.

Onomatopoeia

Objective: The students will use onomatopoeia to create emphasis in descriptive writing.

Procedures

1. Write a definition of onomatopoeia on the chalkboard: *Onomatopoeia is the use of words that sound like things they are describing, such as thwack, snap, buzz, bang, clang, slap, snap,* etc.

2. Read "Example of a Description of Setting" (page 10) and have the students identify the onomatopoeia in the writing.

3. Have the students brainstorm topics for their descriptive writing and write rough drafts. Instruct the students to go through their rough drafts and highlight places where they think that onomatopoeia would be particularly effective.

4. Have the students choose two of the places that they highlighted and add onomatopoeia.

5. Divide the students into partners and have the students share the onomatopoeia that they have added with their partner. Direct them to discuss the following questions: Does the use of onomatopoeia create emphasis and enhance the descriptive writing? What needs to be added, changed, or deleted to improve the writer's use of onomatopoeia?

7. Allow students time to make revisions to their drafts based on their peer's feedback.

Portfolio Piece: Have the students write a reflection in which they identify how their writing is enhanced by onomatopoeia.

Publishing: Have the students share their writing in a round-robin fashion and offer praise for using onomatopoeia.

Technology Connection: Have the students use a word-processing program to revise their descriptive writing.

Home-School Connection: Instruct the students to read an example of descriptive writing with a family member and look for examples of onomatopoeia in the writing.

Assessment: Evaluate students' descriptive writing for the effective use of onomatopoeia.

Hyperbole

Objective: The students will use hyperbole to create emphasis in descriptive writing.

Procedure

1. Write a definition of hyperbole on the chalkboard: *Hyperbole is the use of exaggeration to describe something by stretching the truth in a colorful way.*

2. Read "Example of a Description of Character" (page 11) and have the students identify the hyperbole in the writing. Ask the students to identify other places in the text where hyperbole might be effective.

3. Have the students brainstorm topics for their descriptive writing and write rough drafts. Instruct the students to go through their rough drafts and highlight places where they think that hyperbole would be particularly effective.

4. Have the students complete "Using Hyperbole" (page 67) and add at least one hyperbole to their drafts.

5. Divide the students into partners and have the students share the hyperbole that they have added with their partner. Direct them to discuss the following questions: Does the use of hyperbole enhance the descriptive writing? Explain. What needs to be added, changed, or deleted to improve the writer's use of hyperbole?

6. Allow students time to revise their drafts based on their peer's feedback.

Portfolio Piece: Have the students write a reflection in which they identify how their writing is enhanced by hyperbole.

Publishing: Post the students' writing on a bulletin board with their use of hyperbole highlighted. Read some tall tales to the students and then sprinkle the bulletin board with quotations.

Technology Connection: Have the students use a word-processing program to revise their descriptive writing.

Home-School Connection: Have the students compose a family tall tale and highlight the hyperbole.

Assessment:

1. Assess the students' ability to complete the reproducible entitled "Using Hyperbole."

2. Evaluate students' descriptive writing for the effective use of hyperbole.

Using Hyperbole

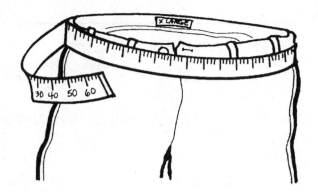

Directions: Read the following information and complete each of the activities. Remember that hyperbole is the use of exaggeration to describe something by stretching the truth in a colorful way.

Examples: The man was wearing pants that were 67 sizes too big.

My mouth was on fire after eating the salsa.

Writer's Practice:

Read each of the sentences below and generate a hyperbole that expresses the intent of the sentence.

1. The wind blew very hard. _____

   _____

2. It took a long time for us to reach our destination. _____

   _____

3. The girl was very funny. _____

   _____

4. The sun was very hot. _____

   _____

5. The house was very big. _____

   _____

Adding to Your Draft:

Find three places in your draft where you have a statement that could easily be turned into hyperbole. Generate a hyperbole for each statement; then select your favorite hyperbole.

Old Sentence	New Sentence with Hyperbole	Check (✔) if adding a hyperbole.

Personification

Objective: The students will use personification to create emphasis in descriptive writing.

Procedure

1. Write a definition of personification on the chalkboard: *Personification is a literary device that gives human traits to non-living things.*

2. Read "Example of a Description of Action" (page 12) and have the students identify the personification in the writing. Ask the students to identify other places in the text where personification would be effective.

3. Have the students brainstorm topics for their descriptive writing and write rough drafts.

4. Review "Using Personification" (page 69) with the students. Instruct students to go through their drafts in the manner described on the worksheet.

5. Divide the students into partners and have the students share the personification that they have added with their partner. Have the students discuss the following questions: How does the use of personification enhance the descriptive writing? What needs to be added, changed, or deleted to improve the writer's use of personification?

6. Allow students time to make revisions to their drafts based on their peer's feedback.

Portfolio Piece: Have the students write a reflection in which they identify the greatest challenge they faced when adding personification to their descriptive writing.

Publishing: Have the students share their writing in a round-robin fashion and offer praise to each other concerning the personification that was added.

Technology Connection: Have the students use a word-processing program to revise their descriptive writing.

Home-School Connection: Have the students play a game with a family member in which the family member names a non-living object and the students have to create an example of personification involving the object.

Assessment:

1. Assess the students' ability to complete the reproducible entitled "Using Personification."

2. Evaluate students' descriptive writing for the effective use of personification.

Using Personification

Directions: Read the following information and complete each of the activities. Remember that personification is a literary device that gives human traits to non-living things.

Examples:

- The volcano wheezed and coughed before it erupted.
- The wind sang a soft lullaby as it blew through the trees.

Writer's Practice:

Create a statement that includes personification for each of the non-living things listed below.

1. Ocean _____

2. Thunder _____

3. Snowstorm _____

Adding to Your Draft:

Find three places in your draft where you have written about a non-living thing and personification could be added. Add personification to the sentence and then select your favorite example of personification and add this example to your draft.

Non-living thing	New Sentence with Personification	Check (✔) if adding personification.
_____	_____ _____	
_____	_____ _____	
_____	_____ _____	

Word Choice for Descriptive Writing

Objective: The student will use specific nouns, descriptive adjectives, vivid verbs, and detailed examples to make the topic appealing to the reader.

Procedure

1. Present the students with the following guidelines for writing descriptively: *Descriptive language uses the following: a) specific nouns, b) descriptive adjectives, c) vivid verbs, and d) detailed examples.*

2. Distribute "Word Choice for Descriptive Writing" (page 71). Read the example of descriptive writing in italics. Ask the students: Does this example use all of the criteria for descriptive language? How do you know?

3. Read "Example of a Description of Character" (page 11) and ask the students to listen for criteria of descriptive writing. Discuss instances in which the piece met the criteria.

4. Direct students to complete "Word Choice for Descriptive Writing." Identify words and/or phrases that are examples of the criteria for descriptive writing.

5. Have students write descriptive paragraphs and analyze them for criteria of descriptive language.

6. Divide students into partners and have them read each other's descriptive writing and analyze them for criteria for descriptive writing.

Portfolio Piece: Have the students highlight specific word choices and then write a prediction about how their use of language will affect the reader.

Publishing: Post student-generated word lists of specific nouns, descriptive adjectives, and vivid verbs for student reference.

Technology Connection: Use a word-processing program to edit and revise for specific word choices.

Home-School Connection: Have students create a cartoon with a family member in which they use specific nouns, descriptive adjectives, and vivid verbs.

Assessment:

1. Evaluate the students' use of the criteria for descriptive writing by reading their writing and looking for the criteria.

2. Evaluate the students' completed worksheets for completeness and accuracy.

Word Choice for Descriptive Writing *(cont.)*

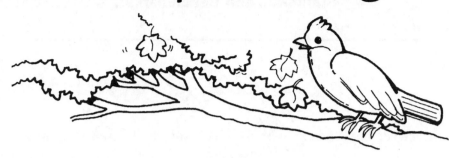

Descriptive writing has . . .

- specific nouns
- descriptive adjectives
- vivid verbs
- detailed examples

Directions: Read the piece of descriptive writing below and complete the chart.

The brilliant azure sky enveloped the world in front of me like a soft blanket. A red cardinal flew overhead, chirping a delightful song before resting in a vibrant, red maple tree. The soft breeze blew through my hair causing me to close my eyes and drink in the beauty of the day. As I opened my eyes, I saw the billowy clouds gently drift across the sky. I longed to climb upon one of those clouds and float into the heavens beyond.

Specific Nouns	Descriptive Adjectives	Vivid Verbs	Detailed Examples
_____	_____	_____	_____
_____	_____	_____	_____
_____	_____	_____	_____
_____	_____	_____	_____
_____	_____	_____	_____
_____	_____	_____	_____
_____	_____	_____	_____
_____	_____	_____	_____
_____	_____	_____	_____
_____	_____	_____	_____
_____	_____	_____	_____

Using Vivid Verbs

Objective: The students will use vivid verbs in descriptive writing to enhance the meaning of the text.

Procedure

1. Have the students brainstorm some action verbs such as talk, laugh, jump, hide, swim, swing, and climb.

2. Pass out "Using Vivid Verbs" (page 73). Review with the students the complete definition of verbs. Have the students complete Parts A and B of the "Writer's Practice" section.

3. Have the students take out drafts of descriptive writing and highlight all of the verbs. Instruct the students to replace ordinary verbs with vivid verbs that specifically express their intent as writers.

4. Instruct the students to switch papers with a peer and to brainstorm vivid verbs to replace ordinary ones.

5. Have the students create a vivid verbs word bank to keep in their notebooks for reference.

Portfolio Piece: Have the students write reflections on the importance of using vivid verbs. Then have them list five ways that they can improve their use of verbs, including highlighting and replacing them; getting a peer to help; referring to the word bank; using a dictionary or thesaurus; and asking the teacher for assistance.

Publishing: Create a vivid verb tree on a bulletin board. Give each student five green paper leaves and tell the students to write a vivid verb on one leaf every night for a week. At the end of the week, assemble a verb tree on the bulletin board.

Technology Connection: Have the students use the thesaurus function to look up additional synonyms for ordinary verbs.

Home-School Connection: Instruct the students to read a descriptive piece of writing in a magazine or literature anthology with a family member and change five ordinary verbs to vivid verbs.

Assessment:

1. Evaluate the students' understanding of vivid verbs by checking "Using Vivid Verbs" for completeness and accuracy.

2. Read the students' descriptive writing and determine if they have applied their knowledge of vivid verbs to their writing.

Using Vivid Verbs *(cont.)*

Directions: Read the information below and then complete the "Writer's Practice" section below. Recall that a verb is a word that shows action or expresses a state of being. A sentence must have a verb in order to be complete. Also, an action verb shows action by telling what someone or something does. The action can be physical (such as jumping, running, climbing) or emotional/mental (such as reflecting, dreaming, loving).

Writer's Practice:

Part A. Complete the following sentences with vivid action verbs.

1. The boy _____ the ball out of the baseball park.

2. The trees _____ in the wind as the storm quickly approached.

3. The fox _____ across the road in an effort to escape unnoticed.

4. The bluebird _____ as it sat on the fence.

5. The girl _____ down the street after the mailman.

Part B. Brainstorm three vivid verbs for each of the following ordinary verbs listed below.

Ordinary Verbs	Vivid Verbs
go	
eat	
said	
sing	
think	

Using End Marks Correctly

Objective: The students will use end marks correctly in all forms of descriptive writing.

Procedure

1. Inform the students they will be learning how to use correct end marks for sentences. Review the three kinds of end marks: periods, exclamation points, and question marks.

2. Distribute and review "Using End Marks" (page 75). Direct the students to complete the "Writer's Practice" section.

3. Have the students reread the descriptive writing that they have composed and determine if they have used end marks correctly.

4. Instruct students to switch papers with a partner. Have them read each other's papers and determine correctness of end marks. Students should make editing changes directly on their papers.

5. Have students compose sentences without proper end marks. Instruct the students to switch papers with a peer and punctuate the student-generated sentences.

Portfolio Piece: Have the students include a reflection in their portfolio in which they identify the importance of using end marks correctly.

Publishing: Create a bulletin board with a chart that has three different categories: periods, exclamation points, and question marks. Give students colorful sentence strips and have them compose sentences to post in each of the categories.

Technology Connection: Remind students that when they are typing sentences, they need to put two spaces after the end mark of a sentence.

Home-School Connection: Have students read advertisements that come in the mail with a family member. Have the students identify the end marks used in the ads and discuss whether or not the author correctly and appropriately used end marks.

Assessment:

1. Evaluate the students' ability to complete the 14 sentences in the "Writer's Practice" section of the reproducible "Using End Marks."

2. Read the students' letters and determine if they applied their knowledge of end marks to their own writing.

Using End Marks

Directions: Read the information about end marks below. Then punctuate the sentences correctly in the section entitled "Writer's Practice."

Period: Use a period at the end of a statement.

Exclamation Point: Use an exclamation point to express excitement or emphasis for an important point. Exclamation points should be used sparingly.

Question Mark: Use a question mark at the end of a question.

Writer's Practice: Put the correct end mark at the end of each of the following sentences.

1. The sun set on the horizon   Wasn't the sight astonishing

2. When the snowflakes stop falling, we will go to the store

3. Where did you get that beautiful, blue ribbon

4. Hurrah   We can finally go swimming in the ocean since the storm has abated

5. When will the sound of cracking thunder stop frightening me

6. The daffodils are blooming all over the hillside, creating a waving carpet of yellow

7. The gazelles ran smoothly and silently in the distance

8. When will moon escape from behind the clouds

9. Wow   I am impressed with the colorful vibrancy of fall

10. How often will you be able to come over to my house this summer

11. Although I like the refreshing coolness of snow cones, I usually don't like ice cream

12. Why is the wind picking up speed   Will there be a hurricane

13. The puppy scurried under the bushes quickly, hoping that nobody had noticed him

14. I will be glad when this project is over and I feel a sense of accomplishment

Verb Tense

Objective: The students will compose a piece of descriptive writing and use past tense.

Procedure

1. Share with the students the following information about verbs: *The tense of a verb reveals the time that the verb is trying to show the audience.*

2. Have the students brainstorm verbs. As the students share ideas, categorize their verbs into a chart on the chalkboard that has the following categories: past tense, present tense, and future tense.

3. Distribute "Verb Tense" (page 77) and direct the students to complete the "Writer's Practice" section.

4. Instruct the students to compose their descriptive writing in the past tense.

5. During the revision process, instruct the students to go through their descriptive writing and highlight their verbs. Have them change any verbs that are not in past tense.

6. Divide the students into pairs. Have them switch papers and take turns checking their drafts for verbs written in the past tense.

Portfolio Piece: Have the students write a reflection about the greatest challenge they faced when keeping their verbs in the past tense.

Publishing: Create a bulletin board of most commonly used past tense verbs for the students to use as a reference. Post excellent examples of descriptive writing written in past tense on the bulletin board.

Technology Connection: Have students use the grammar check function to make sure they have subject-verb agreement throughout their review.

Home-School Connection: Instruct students to read portions of a literature anthology with a family member, identify all the verbs, and categorize them according to tense.

Assessment:

1. Use the rubric on page 14 to score the students' descriptive writing. Read the students' writing carefully for verbs written in the past tense.

2. Require the students to go back and revise if they have not used past tense verbs correctly.

Verb Tense *(cont.)*

Directions: Read the information below about the present, past, and future tense of verbs. Then complete the "Writer's Practice" section below.

> Verbs in the present tense show action that is happening now.
>
> **Example:** We run through the streets.
>
> Verbs in the past tense show action that happened already.
>
> **Example:** We ran through the streets.
>
> Verbs in the future tense show action that is going to happen in the future.
>
> **Example:** We will be running through the streets.

Writer's Practice: Use each of the past tense verbs below in an original sentence.

1. went _____

   _____

2. skipped _____

   _____

3. viewed _____

   _____

4. thought _____

   _____

5. said _____

   _____

6. played _____

   _____

7. sang _____

   _____

8. ate _____

   _____

9. slept _____

   _____

10. talked _____

    _____

Responding to Prompts for Descriptive Writing

Objective: The students will respond to a prompt for descriptive writing by writing an engaging lead, using descriptive details, and composing a powerful conclusion.

Procedure

1. After using the previous lessons to teach skills, explain to the students that they now will be demonstrating these skills by writing in response to prompts. Show the students an example of the rubric to be used for assessment (page 81).

2. Pass out one of the prompts for descriptive writing and instruct the students to brainstorm on the corresponding "Quick Write."

3. Guide and encourage the students as they develop a piece of writing in response to the prompt.

4. Have students use the corresponding "Peer Response Form" to give each other feedback.

5. Instruct the students to revise and redraft as necessary in order to produce a publishable draft.

6. Select all or some of the following activities for the students:

    a. Provide the students with a variety of prompts and allow them to make choices.

    b. Have the students write their own prompts, switch with classmates, and respond to the student-generated prompts.

Portfolio Piece: Have students respond to many of the prompts and choose their favorite for inclusion in their portfolios. Have them write a reflection in which they defend their choices with examples from the text of the their descriptive writing.

Publishing: Create a class magazine and have the students rotate in the role of editor. Each week a different student will write a descriptive piece of writing.

Technology Connection: Have students post their descriptive writing on the school's Web site.

Home-School Connection: Instruct students to select one of the prompts and brainstorm possible responses with a family member.

Assessment: Use the corresponding rubric for each prompt to evaluate the students' descriptive writing.

A Favorite Childhood Toy

Quick Write: Brainstorm a list of five of your favorite childhood toys.

Prompt: Think about your favorite childhood toy. This toy might be a stuffed animal, a game, a bath toy, a yard toy, a baby doll, or an action figure. You may have enjoyed this toy most when you were very small, in preschool, kindergarten, or early elementary school. Write about your memories of this favorite toy. Be sure to include a detailed description of the toy; the setting in which you enjoyed playing with the toy the most; and any particularly happy, sad, fun, or humorous events that you associate with this toy. Make sure to carefully plan your writing and then read the "Prewriting Guide" below so that you include all of the basic elements of descriptive writing when you begin drafting. Incorporate the "Writer's Challenge" elements that are identified at the bottom of the page.

Tip: Use the "Object Chart" (page 24) for brainstorming.

Prewriting Guide

As you draft your descriptive writing, remember to:

❏ Focus your topic.

❏ Write an engaging lead that "grabs" the reader.

❏ Include sufficient supporting details.

❏ Write a powerful conclusion.

❏ Show an awareness of audience.

❏ Link your ideas by using transitions.

❏ Vary your sentence structure and length.

Writer's Challenge:

In your descriptive writing about your favorite childhood toy include:

❏ A Simile

❏ Specific Nouns

❏ Descriptive Adjectives

A Favorite Childhood Toy *(cont.)*
Peer Response Form

Writer: _____

Peer Responder: _____

Part I. Elements of Descriptive Writing

Directions: Writers read their drafts aloud to peers. When they are finished reading, writers should take notes in the space provided under each peer response question.

1. What is the topic of my descriptive writing? How could my topic be more focused?

   _____

   _____

   _____

2. How could my lead be more engaging to the reader? _____

   _____

   _____

   _____

3. What are the details in my writing? How could I improve the details to more clearly describe my topic?

   _____

   _____

   _____

Part II. Writer's Challenge

1. What is my simile? _____

2. Identify some of my descriptive adjectives. _____

3. Identify some of my specific nouns. _____

4. How could I do a better job meeting the Writer's Challenge? _____

   _____

Part III. Writer's Self-Reflection

What information from my peer was particularly useful? _____

_____

_____

_____

A Favorite Childhood Toy *(cont.)*
Rubric

Directions: Use the following rubric to evaluate descriptive writing.

I. Elements of Descriptive Writing

	Self	Peer	Teacher
1. The topic is focused. (2)			
2. The lead is engaging and "grabs" the reader. (4)			
3. Supporting details are sufficient. (4)			
4. The conclusion is powerful. (4)			
5. An awareness of audience is evident. (2)			
6. Transitions link ideas. (3)			
7. Sentence structure is varied. (3)			
8. Sentence length is varied. (3)			
Total points out of 25			

II. Writer's Challenge

	Self	Peer	Teacher
1. One simile (1)			
2. Evidence of descriptive adjectives (4)			
3. Evidence of specific nouns (5)			
Total points out of 10			

III. Teacher's Comments:

_____

_____

_____

_____

_____

A Favorite Friend

Quick Write: Identify five of your favorite friends.

Prompt: Think about a favorite friend. Write a detailed description of your friend and be sure to include details about your friend's physical appearance, the setting in which you usually spend time with this friend, and any particularly happy, sad, fun, or humorous events that you associate with this friend. Incorporate into your description any memories that you have of this friend that help to create a picture of your friend in the reader's mind. Make sure to carefully plan your writing and then read the "Prewriting Guide" below so that you include all of the basic elements of descriptive writing when you begin drafting. Incorporate the "Writer's Challenge" elements that are identified at the bottom of the page.

Tip: Use the "Character Chart" (page 21) to plan your writing.

Prewriting Guide

As you draft your descriptive writing, remember to:

- ❏ Focus your topic.
- ❏ Write an engaging lead that "grabs" the reader.
- ❏ Include sufficient supporting details.
- ❏ Write a powerful conclusion.
- ❏ Show an awareness of audience.
- ❏ Link your ideas by using transitions.
- ❏ Vary your sentence structure and length.

Writer's Challenge

In your descriptive writing about your favorite friend include:

- ❏ A Metaphor
- ❏ Repetition
- ❏ Evidence of Careful Observation

A Favorite Friend *(cont.)*

Peer Response Form

Writer: _____

Peer Responder: _____

Part I. Elements of Descriptive Writing

Directions: Writers read their drafts aloud to peers. When they are finished reading, writers should take notes in the space provided under each peer response question.

1. How could my lead be more engaging to the reader? _____

   _____

   _____

2. What are the details in my writing? How could my details more clearly describe my topic?

   _____

   _____

3. How have I shown an understanding of the audience? Give specific information from the text.

   _____

   _____

Part II. Writer's Challenge

1. What is my metaphor? _____

2. Where in my writing is there evidence of careful observation of my friend? _____

   _____

3. How could I do a better job meeting the Writer's Challenge? _____

   _____

   _____

Part III. Writer's Self-Reflection

What information from my peer was particularly useful? _____

_____

_____

_____

_____

A Favorite Friend (cont.)
Rubric

Directions: Use the following rubric to evaluate descriptive writing.

I. Elements of Descriptive Writing

	Self	Peer	Teacher
1. The topic is focused. (2)			
2. The lead is engaging and "grabs" the reader. (4)			
3. Supporting details are sufficient. (4)			
4. The conclusion is powerful. (4)			
5. An awareness of audience is evident. (2)			
6. Transitions link ideas. (3)			
7. Sentence structure is varied. (3)			
8. Sentence length is varied. (3)			
Total points out of 25			

II. Writer's Challenge

	Self	Peer	Teacher
1. One metaphor (1)			
2. Evidence of repetition (4)			
3. Evidence of careful observation (5)			
Total points out of 10			

III. Writer's Evaluation

My strengths in my writing are _____

_____

_____

My weaknesses in my writing are _____

_____

_____

A Favorite Meal

Quick Write: Brainstorm five of your favorite meals.

Prompt: Think about your favorite meal. Write a description of this favorite meal. In your writing, be sure to include details about the color, shape, and texture of the food. Incorporate into your description information about the people with whom you usually enjoy the meal, the setting in which you eat the meal, and any memories or special events that you associate with the meal. Remember to create a picture of this favorite meal in the reader's mind. You want the reader to be able to taste the meal! Make sure to carefully plan your writing and then read the "Prewriting Guide" below so that you include all of the basic elements of descriptive writing when you begin drafting. Incorporate the "Writer's Challenge" elements that are identified at the bottom of the page.

Prewriting Guide

As you draft your descriptive writing, remember to:

❑ Focus your topic.

❑ Write an engaging lead that "grabs" the reader.

❑ Include sufficient supporting details.

❑ Write a powerful conclusion.

❑ Show an awareness of audience.

❑ Link your ideas by using transitions.

❑ Vary your sentence structure and length.

Writer's Challenge

In your descriptive writing about your favorite meal include:

❑ Rhetorical question

❑ Hyperbole

❑ Descriptive adjectives

A Favorite Meal *(cont.)*
Peer Response Form

Writer: _____

Peer Responder: _____

Part I. Elements of Descriptive Writing

Directions: Writers read their drafts aloud to peers. When they are finished reading, writers should take notes in the space provided under each peer response question.

1. What is the topic of my descriptive writing? How could my topic be more focused?

   _____

   _____

   _____

2. How have I shown an understanding of the audience? Give specific information from the text.

   _____

   _____

   _____

Part II. Writer's Challenge

1. What is my rhetorical question? _____

   _____

2. What is my hyperbole? _____

   _____

3. Identify some of my descriptive adjectives. _____

   _____

4. How could I do a better job meeting the "Writer's Challenge"? _____

   _____

   _____

Part III. Writer's Self-Reflection

How could I improve my listening skills during the peer conference? _____

   _____

   _____

   _____

A Favorite Friend *(cont.)*
Rubric

Directions: Use the following rubric to evaluate descriptive writing.

I. Elements of Descriptive Writing

	Self	Peer	Teacher
1. The topic is focused. (2)			
2. The lead is engaging and "grabs" the reader. (4)			
3. Supporting details are sufficient. (4)			
4. The conclusion is powerful. (4)			
5. An awareness of audience is evident. (2)			
6. Transitions link ideas. (3)			
7. Sentence structure is varied. (3)			
8. Sentence length is varied. (3)			

Total points out of 25

II. Writer's Challenge

	Self	Peer	Teacher
1. A rhetorical question (1)			
2. A hyperbole (1)			
3. Evidence of descriptive adjectives (3)			

Total points out of 5

III. Writer's Evaluation

My work habits throughout the writing process were _____

_____

_____

Specific examples of my work habits include: _____

_____

_____

Bedroom Description

Quick Write: Identify five objects in your bedroom.

Prompt: Think about your bedroom. Write a description of your bedroom, and in your writing, be sure to include details about the color, furniture, decorations, and atmosphere of your bedroom. Incorporate into your description information about any favorite conversations, events, or memories that you associate with your bedroom. Remember to create a picture of your bedroom in the reader's mind. You want the reader to be able to see the curtains, bedspread, window, desk, closet, and any other specific details about your room!

Make sure to carefully plan your writing and then read the "Prewriting Guide" below so that you include all of the basic elements of descriptive writing when you begin drafting. Incorporate the "Writer's Challenge" elements that are identified at the bottom of the page.

Tip: Use the "Setting Chart" (page 22) to plan your descriptive writing.

Prewriting Guide

As you draft your descriptive writing, remember to:

❏ Focus your topic.

❏ Write an engaging lead that "grabs" the reader.

❏ Include sufficient supporting details.

❏ Write a powerful conclusion.

❏ Show an awareness of audience.

❏ Link your ideas by using transitions.

❏ Vary your sentence structure and length.

Writer's Challenge

In your descriptive writing about your bedroom include:

❏ Personification

❏ Evidence of Voice

❏ "Imagine that . . ." sentence beginning

Bedroom Description *(cont.)*
Peer Response Form

Writer: _____

Peer Responder: _____

Part I. Elements of Descriptive Writing

Directions: Writers read their drafts aloud to peers. When they are finished reading, writers should take notes in the space provided under each peer response question.

1. How could my lead be more engaging to the reader? _____

   _____

   _____

2. What are the details in my writing? How could my details more clearly describe my topic?

   _____

   _____

3. Which of my transitions is particularly effective? How could I improve my transitions?

   _____

   _____

Part II. Writer's Challenge

1. Where have I used personification? _____

2. Identify evidence of voice in my writing. _____

   _____

3. Did I effectively use an "Imagine that . . ." sentence beginning? _____

4. How could I do a better job meeting the "Writer's Challenge"? _____

   _____

   _____

Part III. Writer's Self-Reflection

How could I improve my note-taking skills during the peer conference? _____

_____

_____

_____

Bedroom Description *(cont.)*
Rubric

Directions: Use the following rubric to evaluate descriptive writing.

I. Elements of Descriptive Writing

	Self	Peer	Teacher
1. The topic is focused. (2)			
2. The lead is engaging and "grabs" the reader. (4)			
3. Supporting details are sufficient. (4)			
4. The conclusion is powerful. (4)			
5. An awareness of audience is evident. (2)			
6. Transitions link ideas. (3)			
7. Sentence structure is varied. (3)			
8. Sentence length is varied. (3)			
Total points out of 25			

II. Writer's Challenge

	Self	Peer	Teacher
1. An example of personification (1)			
2. Evidence of voice (3)			
3. An "Imagine that . . ." sentence beginning (1)			
Total points out of 5			

III. Writer's Evaluation

My goals for improvement include _____

_____

_____

_____

_____

A Scene from Nature

Quick Write: Write down five things that you might see in a nature scene.

Prompt: Observe a nature scene either by journeying to an actual scenic location or by looking carefully at a colorful picture of a nature scene (calendar pictures are useful for this activity). Write a description of this scene; and in your writing, be sure to include details about mountains, rivers, lakes, hills, valleys, trees, and other physical features of the land. Also include a description of the weather, animals, time of day, season, and atmosphere of the setting. Incorporate into your description information about happy, sad, humorous, or fun memories that you associate with this setting. Make sure to carefully plan your writing and then read the "Prewriting Guide" below so that you include all of the basic elements of descriptive writing when you begin drafting. Incorporate the "Writer's Challenge" elements that are identified at the bottom of the page.

Tip: Use the "Setting Chart" (page 22) to plan your descriptive writing.

Prewriting Guide

As you draft your descriptive writing, remember to:

- ❏ Focus your topic.
- ❏ Write an engaging lead that "grabs" the reader.
- ❏ Include sufficient supporting details.
- ❏ Write a powerful conclusion.
- ❏ Show an awareness of audience.
- ❏ Link your ideas by using transitions.
- ❏ Vary your sentence structure and length.

Writer's Challenge

In your descriptive writing about your nature scene include:

- ❏ Onomatopoeia
- ❏ Alliteration
- ❏ Prepositional phrases

A Scene from Nature *(cont.)*
Peer Response Form

Writer: _____

Peer Responder: _____

Part I. Elements of Descriptive Writing

Directions: Writers read their drafts aloud to peers. When they are finished reading, writers should take notes in the space provided under each peer response question.

1. What is the topic of my descriptive writing? How could my topic be more focused?

   _____

   _____

   _____

2. How have I shown an understanding of the audience? Give specific information from the text.

   _____

   _____

   _____

3. Do I have varied sentence structure and length? Give specific examples. _____

   _____

   _____

   _____

Part II. Writer's Challenge

1. Where have I used onomatopoeia? _____

2. Identify alliteration in my writing. _____

3. Give examples of prepositional phrases from my writing. _____

   _____

4. How could I do a better job meeting the "Writer's Challenge"? _____

   _____

Part III. Writer's Self-Reflection

How could I improve my questioning skills during the peer conference? _____

_____

_____

A Scene from Nature *(cont.)*
Rubric

Directions: Use the following rubric to evaluate descriptive writing.

I. Elements of Descriptive Writing

	Self	Peer	Teacher
1. The topic is focused. (2)			
2. The lead is engaging and "grabs" the reader. (4)			
3. Supporting details are sufficient. (4)			
4. The conclusion is powerful. (4)			
5. An awareness of audience is evident. (2)			
6. Transitions link ideas. (3)			
7. Sentence structure is varied. (3)			
8. Sentence length is varied. (3)			
Total points out of 25			

II. Writer's Challenge

	Self	Peer	Teacher
1. One example of onomatopeia (1)			
2. Alliteration (3)			
3. Evidence of prepositional phrases (6)			
Total points out of 10			

III. Writer's Evaluation

Some tips for doing an excellent piece of descriptive writing include _____

_____

_____

_____

_____

A Favorite Character

Quick Write: Brainstorm five favorite characters from TV shows, movies, or books.

Prompt: Think about a favorite character from a TV show, movie, or book. Write a detailed description of this character and be sure to include details about your character's physical appearance, a central setting where the character spends a lot of time, and any similarities or differences between yourself and the character. Incorporate into your description any happy, funny, or sad memories that your character has experienced. Remember, you are trying to create a picture of this character in the reader's mind. Make sure to carefully plan your writing and then read the "Prewriting Guide" below so that you include all of the basic elements of descriptive writing when you begin drafting. Incorporate the "Writer's Challenge" elements that are identified at the bottom of the page.

Tip: Use the Character Chart (page 21) to plan your descriptive writing.

Prewriting Guide

As you draft your descriptive writing, remember to:

- ❏ Focus your topic.
- ❏ Write an engaging lead that "grabs" the reader.
- ❏ Include sufficient supporting details.
- ❏ Write a powerful conclusion.
- ❏ Show an awareness of audience.
- ❏ Link your ideas by using transitions.
- ❏ Vary your sentence structure and length.

Writer's Challenge

In your descriptive writing about your favorite character include:

- ❏ Evidence of voice
- ❏ Specific nouns
- ❏ Vivid verbs

A Favorite Character *(cont.)*
Peer Response Form

Writer: _____

Peer Responder: _____

Part I. Elements of Descriptive Writing

Directions: Writers read their drafts aloud to peers. When they are finished reading, writers should take notes in the space provided under each peer response question.

1. What is the topic of my descriptive writing? How could my topic be more focused?

   _____

   _____

2. What are the details in my writing? How could my details more clearly describe my topic?

   _____

   _____

3. How have I shown an understanding of the audience? Give specific information from the text.

   _____

   _____

Part II. Writer's Challenge

1. Where do I show evidence of voice. _____

   _____

2. Give examples of specific nouns from my writing. _____

3. Give examples of vivid verbs from my writing. _____

   _____

4. How could I do a better job meeting the Writer's Challenge? _____

   _____

Part III. Writer's Self-Reflection

What are the strengths in my descriptive writing?_____

_____

_____

_____

A Favorite Character *(cont.)*
Rubric

Directions: Use the following rubric to evaluate descriptive writing.

I. Elements of Descriptive Writing

		Self	Peer	Teacher
1. The topic is focused.	(2)			
2. The lead is engaging and "grabs" the reader.	(4)			
3. Supporting details are sufficient.	(4)			
4. The conclusion is powerful.	(4)			
5. An awareness of audience is evident.	(2)			
6. Transitions link ideas.	(3)			
7. Sentence structure is varied.	(3)			
8. Sentence length is varied.	(3)			
Total points out of 25				

II. Writer's Challenge

		Self	Peer	Teacher
1. Evidence of voice	(2)			
2. Specific nouns	(4)			
3. Vivid verbs	(4)			
Total points out of 10				

III. Peer's Comments (Switch papers so that the peer can write his or her comments.)

I was impressed by your use of _____

_____

_____

_____

_____

A Favorite Vacation

Quick Write: Brainstorm five details about your favorite vacation.

Prompt: Think about your favorite vacation. Write a description of this vacation, and in your writing, be sure to include details about the journey to the vacation spot, the setting of the vacation, and who participated in the vacation. Be sure to include a description of the weather, season, and atmosphere of your vacation. Incorporate into your description information about happy, sad, humorous, or fun memories that you associate with this vacation.

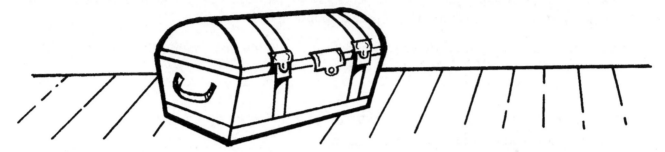

Make sure to carefully plan your writing and then read the "Prewriting Guide" below so that you include all of the basic elements of descriptive writing when you begin drafting. Incorporate the "Writer's Challenge" elements that are identified at the bottom of the page.

Tip: Use the 5 Ws and How Organizer (page 25) to plan your writing.

Prewriting Guide

As you draft your descriptive writing, remember to:

- ❏ Focus your topic.
- ❏ Write an engaging lead that "grabs" the reader.
- ❏ Include sufficient supporting details.
- ❏ Write a powerful conclusion.
- ❏ Show an awareness of audience.
- ❏ Link your ideas by using transitions.
- ❏ Vary your sentence structure and length.

Writer's Challenge

In your descriptive writing about your favorite vacation include:

- ❏ Personification
- ❏ Alliteration
- ❏ Rhetorical question

A Favorite Vacation *(cont.)*
Peer Response Form

Writer: _____

Peer Responder: _____

Part I. Elements of Descriptive Writing

Directions: Writers read their drafts aloud to peers. When they are finished reading, writers should take notes in the space provided under each peer response question.

1. What is the topic of my descriptive writing? How could my topic be more focused?

   _____

   _____

2. How could my lead be more engaging to the reader? _____

   _____

   _____

3. Which of my transitions is particularly effective? How could I improve my transitions?

   _____

   _____

   _____

Part II. Writer's Challenge

1. Identify one example of personification in my writing. _____

   _____

2. Identify one example of alliteration in my writing. _____

3. Identify my rhetorical question. _____

   _____

4. How could I do a better job meeting the "Writer's Challenge"? _____

   _____

Part III. Writer's Self-Reflection

What are two things that I need to do to be a good peer responder to my partner? _____

_____

_____

_____

A Favorite Vacation *(cont.)*
Rubric

Directions: Use the following rubric to evaluate descriptive writing.

I. Elements of Descriptive Writing

	Self	Peer	Teacher
1. The topic is focused. (2)			
2. The lead is engaging and "grabs" the reader. (4)			
3. Supporting details are sufficient. (4)			
4. The conclusion is powerful. (4)			
5. An awareness of audience is evident. (2)			
6. Transitions link ideas. (3)			
7. Sentence structure is varied. (3)			
8. Sentence length is varied. (3)			
Total points out of 25			

II. Writer's Challenge

	Self	Peer	Teacher
1. Personification (1)			
2. Alliteration (3)			
3. Rhetorical question (1)			
Total points out of 5			

III. Peer's Comments: (Switch papers so that the peer can write his or her comments.)

I enjoyed reading the part in your writing where you described _____

_____

_____

_____

_____

Backyard Description

Quick Write: List five things in your backyard.

Prompt: Begin by observing your backyard carefully. Write a description of your backyard; and in your writing, be sure to include details about landscaping, yard furniture, evidence of small creatures and insects, and any physical structures such as a shed or deck. Incorporate into your description information about happy, sad, humorous, or fun memories that you associate with your backyard.

Make sure to carefully plan your writing and then read the "Prewriting Guide" below so that you include all of the basic elements of descriptive writing when you begin drafting. Incorporate the "Writer's Challenge" elements that are identified at the bottom of the page.

Tip: Use the Setting Chart (page 22) to gather information for your descriptive writing.

Prewriting Guide

As you draft your descriptive writing, remember to:

❏ Focus your topic.

❏ Write an engaging lead that "grabs" the reader.

❏ Include sufficient supporting details.

❏ Write a powerful conclusion.

❏ Show an awareness of audience.

❏ Link your ideas by using transitions.

❏ Vary your sentence structure and length.

Writer's Challenge

In your descriptive writing about your backyard include:

❏ Description that creates mood

❏ Hyperbole

❏ Appropriate end marks

Backyard Description *(cont.)*
Peer Response Form

Writer: _____

Peer Responder: _____

Part I. Elements of Descriptive Writing

Directions: Writers read their drafts aloud to peers. When they are finished reading, writers should take notes in the space provided under each peer response question.

1. What is the topic of my descriptive writing? How could my topic be more focused?

   _____

   _____

2. What are the details in my writing? How could my details more clearly describe my topic?

   _____

   _____

3. Do I have varied sentence structure and length? Give specific examples. ___ _____

   _____

   _____

Part II. Writer's Challenge

1. Is there evidence of description that creates mood? Give examples._____

   _____

2. Identify one example of hyperbole in my writing. _____

3. Have I used appropriate end marks? Explain. _____

   _____

4. How could I do a better job meeting the "Writer's Challenge"? _____

   _____

   _____

Part III. Writer's Self-Reflection

What information from my peer was particularly useful? _____

_____

_____

_____

Backyard Description *(cont.)*
Rubric

Directions: Use the following rubric to evaluate descriptive writing.

I. Elements of Descriptive Writing

	Self	Peer	Teacher
1. The topic is focused. (2)			
2. The lead is engaging and "grabs" the reader. (4)			
3. Supporting details are sufficient. (4)			
4. The conclusion is powerful. (4)			
5. An awareness of audience is evident. (2)			
6. Transitions link ideas. (3)			
7. Sentence structure is varied. (3)			
8. Sentence length is varied. (3)			
Total points out of 25			

II. Writer's Challenge

	Self	Peer	Teacher
1. Evidence of mood (4)			
2. Hyperbole (1)			
3. Correct end marks (5)			
Total points out of 5			

III. Peer's Comments: (Switch papers so that the peer can write his or her comments.)

The mood of your writing was _____

_____

_____

_____

_____

A Favorite Animal

Quick Write: Brainstorm three details about a favorite animal. (This animal can be a family pet, a friend's pet, or a character from a TV show or movie.)

Prompt: Think about a favorite animal. Write a detailed description of this animal and be sure to include details about the animal's physical appearance, a central setting where the animal spends a lot of time, and any sounds associated with this animal. Incorporate into your description any happy, funny, or sad memories connected to this animal. Remember that you are trying to create a picture of this animal in the reader's mind. Make sure to carefully plan your writing and then read the "Prewriting Guide" below so that you  include all of the basic elements of descriptive writing when you begin drafting. Incorporate the "Writer's Challenge" elements that are identified at the bottom of the page.

Prewriting Guide

As you draft your descriptive writing, remember to:

❏ Focus your topic.

❏ Write a lead that engages the reader.

❏ Include sufficient supporting details.

❏ Write a powerful conclusion.

❏ Show an awareness of audience.

❏ Link your ideas by using transitions.

❏ Vary your sentence structure and length.

Writer's Challenge

In your descriptive writing about a favorite animal include:

❏ Descriptive adjectives

❏ Vivid verbs

❏ A metaphor

A Favorite Animal *(cont.)*
Peer Response Form

Writer: _____

Peer Responder: _____

Part I. Elements of Descriptive Writing

Directions: Writers read their drafts aloud to peers. When they are finished reading, writers should take notes in the space provided under each peer response question.

1. How could my lead be more engaging to the reader? _____

   _____

   _____

2. What information do I need to add, delete, or change in my conclusion in order to make it more powerful?

   _____

   _____

3. How have I shown an understanding of the audience? Give specific information from the text.

   _____

   _____

Part II. Writer's Challenge

1. Is there evidence of descriptive adjectives? Give examples. _____

   _____

2. Is there evidence of vivid verbs? Give examples. _____

3. What is the metaphor in my writing? _____

   _____

4. How could I do a better job meeting the "Writer's Challenge"? _____

   _____

Part III. Writer's Self-Reflection

What am I going to change about my draft as a result of my peer conference? _____

_____

_____

_____

A Favorite Animal (cont.)
Rubric

Directions: Use the following rubric to evaluate descriptive writing.

I. Elements of Descriptive Writing

	Self	Peer	Teacher
1. The topic is focused. (2)			
2. The lead is engaging and "grabs" the reader. (4)			
3. Supporting details are sufficient. (4)			
4. The conclusion is powerful. (4)			
5. An awareness of audience is evident. (2)			
6. Transitions link ideas. (3)			
7. Sentence structure is varied. (3)			
8. Sentence length is varied. (3)			
Total points out of 25			

II. Writer's Challenge

	Self	Peer	Teacher
1. Descriptive adjectives (5)			
2. Vivid verbs (4)			
3. A metaphor (1)			
Total points out of 10			

III. Peer's Comments: (Switch papers so that the peer can write his or her comments.)

You used excellent descriptive detail when you wrote _____

_____

_____

_____

A Favorite Teacher

Quick Write: Brainstorm four character traits of your favorite teacher.

Prompt: Think about a favorite teacher. Write a detailed description of your teacher and be sure to include details about your teacher's physical appearance, the subject and grade level that he/she teaches, and details about your favorite teacher's classroom. Incorporate into your description any particularly happy, sad, fun, or humorous events that you associate with this teacher. Be sure to include memories that you have of this teacher that help to create a picture of your teacher in the reader's mind.

Make sure to carefully plan your writing and then read the "Prewriting Guide" below so that you include all of the basic elements of descriptive writing when you begin drafting. Incorporate the "Writer's Challenge" elements that are identified at the bottom of the page.

Tip: Use the Character Chart (page 21) to plan your descriptive writing.

Prewriting Guide

As you draft your descriptive writing, remember to:

- ❏ Focus your topic.
- ❏ Write an engaging lead that "grabs" the reader.
- ❏ Include sufficient supporting details.
- ❏ Write a powerful conclusion.
- ❏ Show an awareness of audience.
- ❏ Link your ideas by using transitions.
- ❏ Vary your sentence structure and length.

Writer's Challenge

In your descriptive writing about your favorite teacher include:

- ❏ Evidence of voice
- ❏ "Imagine that . . ." sentence beginning
- ❏ A simile

A Favorite Teacher *(cont.)*
Peer Response Form

Writer: _____

Peer Responder: _____

Part I. Elements of Descriptive Writing

Directions: Writers read their drafts aloud to peers. When they are finished reading, writers should take notes in the space provided under each peer response question.

1. What is the topic of my descriptive writing? How could my topic be more focused?

   _____

   _____

   _____

2. What are the details in my writing? How could my details more clearly describe my topic?

   _____

   _____

   _____

3. Do I have varied sentence structure and length? Give specific examples. _____

   _____

   _____

   _____

Part II. Writer's Challenge

1. Is there evidence of voice? Give examples. _____

   _____

2. What is the simile in my writing? _____

   _____

Part III. Writer's Self-Reflection

How could I improve my listening skills during the peer conference? _____

_____

_____

_____

A Favorite Teacher *(cont.)*
Rubric

Directions: Use the following rubric to evaluate descriptive writing.

I. Elements of Descriptive Writing

	Self	Peer	Teacher
1. The topic is focused. (2)			
2. The lead is engaging and "grabs" the reader. (4)			
3. Supporting details are sufficient. (4)			
4. The conclusion is powerful. (4)			
5. An awareness of audience is evident. (2)			
6. Transitions link ideas. (3)			
7. Sentence structure is varied. (3)			
8. Sentence length is varied. (3)			
Total points out of 25			

II. Writer's Challenge

	Self	Peer	Teacher
1. Evidence of voice (3)			
2. "Imagine that . . ." sentence beginning (1)			
3. A simile (1)			
Total points out of 5			

III. Peer's Comments: (Switch papers so that the peer can write his or her comments.)

When reading your descriptive writing, I gained a better understanding of how to_____

_____

_____

_____

_____

The Family Car

Quick Write: List five details that could be used to describe the family car.

Prompt: Think about the family car. (If your family owns more than one car, choose one car to describe.) Write a description of your car and make sure to include the color, make, model, and special features of the car. Incorporate into this description any memories associated with the car including special destinations and people who have traveled in the car with you. Be sure to include any particularly happy, sad, fun, or humorous events that are connected with the family car. Make sure to carefully plan your writing and then read the "Prewriting Guide" below so that you include all of the basic elements of descriptive writing when you begin drafting. Incorporate the "Writer's Challenge" elements that are identified at the bottom of the page.

Tip: Use the Object Chart (page 24) to plan your descriptive writing.

Prewriting Guide

As you draft your descriptive writing, remember to:

- ❏ Focus your topic.
- ❏ Write an engaging lead that "grabs" the reader.
- ❏ Include sufficient supporting details.
- ❏ Write a powerful conclusion.
- ❏ Show an awareness of audience.
- ❏ Link your ideas by using transitions.
- ❏ Vary your sentence structure and length.

Writer's Challenge

In your descriptive writing about the family car include:

- ❏ Repetition
- ❏ Assonance
- ❏ Evidence of careful observation

The Family Car *(cont.)*
Peer Response Form

Writer: _____

Peer Responder: _____

Part I. Elements of Descriptive Writing

Directions: Writers read their drafts aloud to peers. When they are finished reading, writers should take notes in the space provided under each peer response question.

1. What is the topic of my descriptive writing? How could my topic be more focused?

   _____

   _____

   _____

2. How have I shown an understanding of the audience? Give specific information from the text.

   _____

   _____

   _____

3. Which of my transitions is particularly effective? How could I improve my transitions?

   _____

   _____

   _____

Part II. Writer's Challenge

1. What is the repetition in my descriptive writing? _____

   _____

2. Identify the example of assonance in my writing. _____

   _____

3. Is there evidence of careful observation in my writing? Explain. _____

   _____

Part III. Writer's Self-Reflection

How could I improve my note-taking skills during the peer conference? _____

_____

_____

The Family Car *(cont.)*
Rubric

Directions: Use the following rubric to evaluate descriptive writing.

I. Elements of Descriptive Writing

	Self	Peer	Teacher
1. The topic is focused. (2)			
2. The lead is engaging and "grabs" the reader. (4)			
3. Supporting details are sufficient. (4)			
4. The conclusion is powerful. (4)			
5. An awareness of audience is evident. (2)			
6. Transitions link ideas. (3)			
7. Sentence structure is varied. (3)			
8. Sentence length is varied. (3)			
Total points out of 25			

II. Writer's Challenge

	Self	Peer	Teacher
1. Repetition (3)			
2. Assonance (1)			
3. Evidence of careful observation (6)			
Total points out of 10			

III. Writer's Evaluation

My work habits throughout the writing process were_____

_____

_____

My goals for improvement include _____

_____

_____

A Recent Sports Event

Quick Write: List three of your favorite sports.

Prompt: Think about a recent sports event. Write a description of this sports event, and in your writing, include relevant details about the journey to the event, the kind of sport, the setting in which the sport took place, and who participated in the sport. Be sure to include a description of the weather, season, and competitive atmosphere of the sport. Incorporate into your description memories of action, anticipation, and excitement associated with the sporting event. Make sure to carefully plan your writing and then read the "Prewriting Guide" below so that you include all of the basic elements of descriptive writing when you begin drafting. Incorporate the "Writer's Challenge" elements that are identified at the bottom of the page.

Tip: Use the Action Chart (page 23) to gather ideas for your description.

Prewriting Guide

As you draft your descriptive writing, remember to:

- ❑ Focus your topic.
- ❑ Write an engaging lead that "grabs" the reader.
- ❑ Include sufficient supporting details.
- ❑ Write a powerful conclusion.
- ❑ Show an awareness of audience.
- ❑ Link your ideas by using transitions.
- ❑ Vary your sentence structure and length.

Writer's Challenge

In your descriptive writing about a recent sports event include:

- ❑ A simile
- ❑ Vivid verbs
- ❑ Evidence of voice

A Recent Sports Event *(cont.)*

Peer Response Form

Writer: _____

Peer Responder: _____

Part I. Elements of Descriptive Writing

Directions: Writers read their drafts aloud to peers. When they are finished reading, writers should take notes in the space provided under each peer response question.

1. How could my lead be more engaging to the reader? _____

_____

_____

2. How could my details more clearly describe my topic? _____

_____

_____

3. What information do I need to add, delete, or change in my conclusion in order to make it more powerful?

_____

_____

Part II. Writer's Challenge

1. What is the simile in my descriptive writing? _____

_____

2. Identify examples of vivid verbs in my writing. _____

_____

3. Is there evidence of voice in my writing? Explain. _____

_____

Part III. Writer's Self-Reflection

What are the weaknesses in my descriptive writing? _____

_____

_____

_____

_____

A Recent Sports Event *(cont.)*
Rubric

Directions: Use the following rubric to evaluate descriptive writing.

I. Elements of Descriptive Writing

	Self	Peer	Teacher
1. The topic is focused. (2)			
2. The lead is engaging and "grabs" the reader. (4)			
3. Supporting details are sufficient. (4)			
4. The conclusion is powerful. (4)			
5. An awareness of audience is evident. (2)			
6. Transitions link ideas. (3)			
7. Sentence structure is varied. (3)			
8. Sentence length is varied. (3)			
Total points out of 25			

II. Writer's Challenge

	Self	Peer	Teacher
1. One simile (1)			
2. Vivid verbs (4)			
3. Evidence of voice (5)			
Total points out of 10			

III. Writer's Evaluation

My topic was (interesting, not interesting) to me because _____

_____

_____

_____

_____

A Musical Event

Quick Write: Brainstorm five of your favorite songs.

Prompt: Think about a recent musical event. (This may be an event in which you participated or an event where you were a member of the audience.) Write a description of this musical event; and in your writing, include relevant details about the tempo and rhythm of the music, the setting for the musical event, and who participated in the event. Be sure to include words and phrases that create an image of the mood associated with the  event. Incorporate into your description memories of anticipation and excitement associated with the musical event. Make sure to carefully plan your writing and then read the "Prewriting Guide" below so that you include all of the basic elements of descriptive writing when you begin drafting. Incorporate the "Writer's Challenge" elements that are identified at the bottom of the page.

Prewriting Guide

As you draft your descriptive writing, remember to:

❑ Focus your topic.

❑ Write an engaging lead that "grabs" the reader.

❑ Include sufficient supporting details.

❑ Write a powerful conclusion.

❑ Show an awareness of audience.

❑ Link your ideas by using transitions.

❑ Vary your sentence structure and length.

Writer's Challenge

In your descriptive writing about a musical event include:

❑ Imagery

❑ Repetition

❑ Onomatopoeia

A Musical Event *(cont.)*
Peer Response Form

Writer: _____

Peer Responder: _____

Part I. Elements of Descriptive Writing

Directions: Writers read their drafts aloud to peers. When they are finished reading, writers should take notes in the space provided under each peer response question.

1. What is the topic of my descriptive writing? How could my topic be more focused?

   _____

   _____

   _____

2. How could my lead be more engaging to the reader?_____

   _____

   _____

3. How could my details more clearly describe my topic? _____

   _____

   _____

Part II. Writer's Challenge

1. Give examples of the imagery in my writing. _____

   _____

2. Identify an example of repetition in my writing. _____

   _____

3. Identify the onomatopoeia in my writing._____

   _____

Part III. Writer's Self-Reflection

How could I improve my listening skills during the peer conference? _____

_____

_____

_____

_____

A Musical Event (*cont.*)
Rubric

Directions: Use the following rubric to evaluate descriptive writing.

I. Elements of Descriptive Writing

	Self	Peer	Teacher
1. The topic is focused. (2)			
2. The lead is engaging and "grabs" the reader. (4)			
3. Supporting details are sufficient. (4)			
4. The conclusion is powerful. (4)			
5. An awareness of audience is evident. (2)			
6. Transitions link ideas. (3)			
7. Sentence structure is varied. (3)			
8. Sentence length is varied. (3)			
Total points out of 25			

II. Writer's Challenge

	Self	Peer	Teacher
1. Imagery (4)			
2. Repetition (3)			
3. Onomatopeia (3)			
Total points out of 5			

III. Writer's Evaluation

My strengths in my writing are _____

_____

_____

My weaknesses in my writing are _____

_____

_____

A Thunderstorm

Quick Write: List five sensory details that you associate with a thunderstorm.

Prompt: Think about a recent thunderstorm. Write a description of this thunderstorm, and in your writing, include relevant details about the thunder, lightening, and the tempo and rhythm of the rain. Include information about the setting of the thunderstorm and the people or pets that you were with during the thunderstorm. Be sure to include words and phrases that create an image of the mood associated with the thunderstorm. Incorporate into your description memories of anxiety, apprehension, and/or excitement associated with the thunderstorm. Make sure to carefully plan your writing and then read the "Prewriting Guide" below so that you include all of the basic elements of descriptive writing when you begin drafting. Incorporate the "Writer's Challenge" elements identified at the bottom of the page.

Prewriting Guide

As you draft your descriptive writing, remember to:

- ❏ Focus your topic.
- ❏ Write an engaging lead that "grabs" the reader.
- ❏ Include sufficient supporting details.
- ❏ Write a powerful conclusion.
- ❏ Show an awareness of audience.
- ❏ Link your ideas by using transitions.
- ❏ Vary your sentence structure and length.

Writer's Challenge

In your descriptive writing about a thunderstorm include:

- ❏ Mood
- ❏ Descriptive adjectives
- ❏ Vivid verbs

A Thunderstorm *(cont.)*
Peer Response Form

Writer: _____

Peer Responder: _____

Part I. Elements of Descriptive Writing

Directions: Writers read their drafts aloud to peers. When they are finished reading, writers should take notes in the space provided under each peer response question.

1. What is the topic of my descriptive writing? How could my topic be more focused?

   _____

   _____

   _____

2. What are the details in my writing? How could my details more clearly describe my topic?

   _____

   _____

   _____

3. How have I shown an understanding of the audience? _____

   _____

   _____

   _____

Part II. Writer's Challenge

1. What are some words and phrases that enhance the mood of the writing? _____

   _____

2. Identify examples of descriptive adjectives in my writing. _____

   _____

3. Identify examples of vivid verbs. Explain. _____

   _____

Part III. Writer's Self-Reflection

What am I going to change about my draft as a result of my peer conference? _____

_____

_____

A Thunderstorm *(cont.)*
Rubric

Directions: Use the following rubric to evaluate descriptive writing.

I. Elements of Descriptive Writing

	Self	Peer	Teacher
1. The topic is focused. (2)			
2. The lead is engaging and "grabs" the reader. (4)			
3. Supporting details are sufficient. (4)			
4. The conclusion is powerful. (4)			
5. An awareness of audience is evident. (2)			
6. Transitions link ideas. (3)			
7. Sentence structure is varied. (3)			
8. Sentence length is varied. (3)			
Total points out of 25			

II. Writer's Challenge

	Self	Peer	Teacher
1. Evidence of mood (4)			
2. Evidence of descriptive adjectives (3)			
3. Vivid verbs (3)			
Total points out of 10			

III. Teacher's Comment:

_____

_____

_____

_____

_____

A Snowstorm

Quick Write: List five sensory details that describe a snowstorm.

Prompt: Think about a recent snowstorm. Write a description of this snowstorm; and in your writing, include relevant details about the snowflakes, wind gusts, temperature, and color of the sky. Include information about the setting of the snowstorm and the people or pets that you were with during the snowstorm. Be sure to include words and phrases that create an image of the mood associated with the snowstorm. Incorporate into your description memories of excitement and wonder associated with the snowstorm.

Make sure to carefully plan your writing and then read the "Prewriting Guide" below so that you include all of the basic elements of descriptive writing when you begin drafting. Incorporate the "Writer's Challenge" elements that are identified at the bottom of the page.

Prewriting Guide

As you draft your descriptive writing, remember to:

- ❏ Focus your topic.
- ❏ Write an engaging lead that "grabs" the reader.
- ❏ Include sufficient supporting details.
- ❏ Write a powerful conclusion.
- ❏ Show an awareness of audience.
- ❏ Link your ideas by using transitions.
- ❏ Vary your sentence structure and length.

Writer's Challenge

In your descriptive writing about your snowstorm include:

- ❏ Prepositional phrases
- ❏ Rhetorical question
- ❏ Theme

A Snowstorm *(cont.)*
Peer Response Form

Writer: _____

Peer Responder: _____

Part I. Elements of Descriptive Writing

Directions: Writers read their drafts aloud to peers. When they are finished reading, writers should take notes in the space provided under each peer response question.

1. What is the topic of my descriptive writing? How could my topic be more focused?

_____

_____

_____

2. How could my details more clearly describe my topic? _____

_____

_____

_____

3. Do I have varied sentence structure and length? Give specific examples. _____

_____

_____

_____

Part II. Writer's Challenge

1. Identify some of the prepositional phrases in my descriptive writing. _____

_____

2. What is the rhetorical question I have included? _____

_____

3. What is the theme of my snowstorm description? _____

_____

Part III. Writer's Self-Reflection

What information from my peer was particularly useful? _____

_____

_____

_____

A Snowstorm *(cont.)*
Rubric

Directions: Use the following rubric to evaluate descriptive writing.

I. Elements of Descriptive Writing

	Self	Peer	Teacher
1. The topic is focused. (2)			
2. The lead is engaging and "grabs" the reader. (4)			
3. Supporting details are sufficient. (4)			
4. The conclusion is powerful. (4)			
5. An awareness of audience is evident. (2)			
6. Transitions link ideas. (3)			
7. Sentence structure is varied. (3)			
8. Sentence length is varied. (3)			
Total points out of 25			

II. Writer's Challenge

	Self	Peer	Teacher
1. Prepositonal phrases (4)			
2. Rhetorical questions (1)			
3. Incorporation of theme (5)			
Total points out of 5			

III. Writer's Evaluation

Using prepositional phrases enhances my writing because _____

_____

Other ways to enhance descriptive writing include_____

_____

My favorite way to enhance descriptive writing is _____

_____

The Neighborhood

Quick Write: Brainstorm five details about your neighborhood.

Prompt: Begin by observing your neighborhood carefully. Write a description of your neighborhood. In your writing, be sure to include details about landscaping, street signs, style of houses, trees and shrubs, sidewalks, and lawn furniture and other exterior accessories such as signs and lamp posts. Incorporate into your description information about happy, sad, humorous, or fun memories that you associate with your neighborhood.

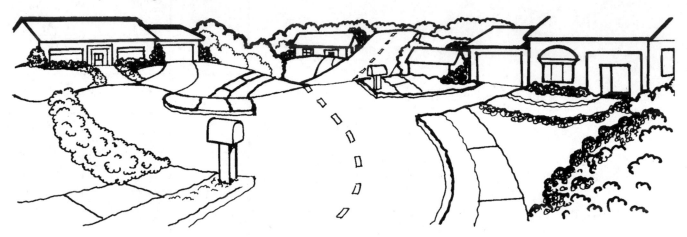

Make sure to carefully plan your writing and then read the "Prewriting Guide" below so that you include all of the basic elements of descriptive writing when you begin drafting. Incorporate the "Writer's Challenge" elements identified at the bottom of the page.

Tip: Use the Setting Chart (page 22) to plan your descriptive writing.

Prewriting Guide

As you draft your descriptive writing, remember to:

- ❏ Focus your topic.
- ❏ Write an engaging lead that "grabs" the reader.
- ❏ Include sufficient supporting details.
- ❏ Write a powerful conclusion.
- ❏ Show an awareness of audience.
- ❏ Link your ideas by using transitions.
- ❏ Vary your sentence structure and length.

Writer's Challenge

In your descriptive writing about your neighborhood include:

- ❏ Evidence of voice
- ❏ Alliteration
- ❏ Descriptive adjectives

The Neighborhood *(cont.)*
Peer Response Form

Writer: _____

Peer Responder: _____

Part I. Elements of Descriptive Writing

Directions: Writers read their drafts aloud to peers. When they are finished reading, writers should take notes in the space provided under each peer response question.

1. How could my lead be more engaging to the reader? _____

   _____

   _____

2. How could my details more clearly describe my topic? _____

   _____

   _____

3. What information do I need to add, delete, or change in my conclusion in order to make it more powerful?

   _____

   _____

Part II. Writer's Challenge

1. Have I given adequate evidence of my voice as a writer? Explain. _____

   _____

2. Identify an example of alliteration in my writing. _____

   _____

3. Identify examples of descriptive adjectives in my writing. _____

   _____

Part III. Writer's Self-Reflection

What am I going to change about my draft as a result of my peer conference? _____

_____

_____

_____

_____

The Neighborhood *(cont.)*
Rubric

Directions: Use the following rubric to evaluate descriptive writing.

I. Elements of Descriptive Writing

	Self	Peer	Teacher
1. The topic is focused. (2)			
2. The lead is engaging and "grabs" the reader. (4)			
3. Supporting details are sufficient. (4)			
4. The conclusion is powerful. (4)			
5. An awareness of audience is evident. (2)			
6. Transitions link ideas. (3)			
7. Sentence structure is varied. (3)			
8. Sentence length is varied. (3)			
Total points out of 25			

II. Writer's Challenge

	Self	Peer	Teacher
1. Evidence of voice (4)			
2. Alliteration (3)			
3. Descriptive adjectives (3)			
Total points out of 5			

III. Writer's Evaluation

I would like to add the following details to my description of my neighborhood:_____

_____

_____

These details would enhance my description because _____

_____

_____

The Classroom

Quick Write: List five descriptive details about your classroom.

Prompt: Begin by observing your classroom carefully. Write a description of your classroom; and in your writing, be sure to include details about bulletin boards, classroom furniture, windows, chalkboards, learning stations, and the teacher's desk. Incorporate into your description information about happy, frustrating, humorous, or fun memories that you associate with your classroom.

Make sure to carefully plan your writing and then read the "Prewriting Guide" below so that you include all of the basic elements of descriptive writing when you begin drafting. Incorporate the "Writer's Challenge" elements identified at the bottom of the page.

Tip: Use the Setting Chart (page 22) to plan your descriptive writing.

Prewriting Guide

As you draft your descriptive writing, remember to:

- ❏ Focus your topic.
- ❏ Write an engaging lead that "grabs" the reader.
- ❏ Include sufficient supporting details.
- ❏ Write a powerful conclusion.
- ❏ Show an awareness of audience.
- ❏ Link your ideas by using transitions.
- ❏ Vary your sentence structure and length.

Writer's Challenge

In your descriptive writing about your classroom include:

- ❏ Hyperbole
- ❏ Repetition
- ❏ Rhetorical Question

The Classroom *(cont.)*
Peer Response Form

Writer: _____

Peer Responder: _____

Part I. Elements of Descriptive Writing

Directions: Writers read their drafts aloud to peers. When they are finished reading, writers should take notes in the space provided under each peer response question.

1. What is the topic of my descriptive writing? How could my topic be more focused?

   _____

   _____

   _____

2. How could my details more clearly describe my topic? _____

   _____

   _____

   _____

3. Which of my transitions is particularly effective? How could I improve my transitions?

   _____

   _____

   _____

Part II. Writer's Challenge

1. What is the hyperbole in my descriptive writing? _____

   _____

2. Identify the example of repetition in my writing. _____

   _____

3. Is my use of a rhetorical question effective? Explain. _____

   _____

Part III. Writer's Self-Reflection

How could I improve my listening skills during the peer conference? _____

_____

_____

_____

The Classroom (cont.)
Rubric

Directions: Use the following rubric to evaluate descriptive writing.

I. Elements of Descriptive Writing

	Self	Peer	Teacher
1. The topic is focused. (2)			
2. The lead is engaging and "grabs" the reader. (4)			
3. Supporting details are sufficient. (4)			
4. The conclusion is powerful. (4)			
5. An awareness of audience is evident. (2)			
6. Transitions link ideas. (3)			
7. Sentence structure is varied. (3)			
8. Sentence length is varied. (3)			

Total points out of 25

II. Writer's Challenge

	Self	Peer	Teacher
1. Hyperbole (1)			
2. Repetition (3)			
3. Rhetorical question (1)			

Total points out of 5

III. Writer's Evaluation

My weaknesses in my writing are _____

_____

_____

My goals for improvement include _____

_____

_____

A Favorite TV Show

Quick Write: List three of your favorite TV shows.

Prompt: Think about your favorite TV show. Write a description of this TV show; and in your writing, include relevant details about the characters, setting, and action of the show. Consider describing the similarities and differences between the main character and you. Incorporate into your description memories of anticipation and excitement associated with watching this TV show. Make sure to carefully plan your writing and then read the "Prewriting Guide" below so that you include all of the basic elements of descriptive writing when you begin drafting. Incorporate the "Writer's Challenge" elements that are identified below.

Prewriting Guide

As you draft your descriptive writing, remember to:

❏ Focus your topic.

❏ Write an engaging lead that "grabs" the reader.

❏ Include sufficient supporting details.

❏ Write a powerful conclusion.

❏ Show an awareness of audience.

❏ Link your ideas by using transitions.

❏ Vary your sentence structure and length.

Writer's Challenge

In your descriptive writing about your favorite TV show include:

❏ A simile

❏ Vivid verbs

❏ Evidence of voice

A Favorite TV Show *(cont.)*
Peer Response Form

Writer: _____

Peer Responder: _____

Part I. Elements of Descriptive Writing

Directions: Writers read their drafts aloud to peers. When they are finished reading, writers should take notes in the space provided under each peer response question.

1. What is the topic of my descriptive writing? How could my topic be more focused?

   _____

   _____

2. What information do I need to add, delete, or change in my conclusion in order to make it more powerful? _____

   _____

   _____

3. How have I shown an understanding of the audience? Give specific information from the text.

   _____

   _____

Part II. Writer's Challenge

1. What is the simile in my descriptive writing? _____

   _____

2. Identify the vivid verbs in my writing. _____

   _____

3. Is there evidence of voice in my writing? Explain. _____

   _____

Part III. Writer's Self-Reflection

How could I improve my questioning skills during the peer conference? _____

_____

_____

_____

A Favorite TV Show *(cont.)*

Rubric

Directions: Use the following rubric to evaluate descriptive writing.

I. Elements of Descriptive Writing

	Self	Peer	Teacher
1. The topic is focused. (2)			
2. The lead is engaging and "grabs" the reader. (4)			
3. Supporting details are sufficient. (4)			
4. The conclusion is powerful. (4)			
5. An awareness of audience is evident. (2)			
6. Transitions link ideas. (3)			
7. Sentence structure is varied. (3)			
8. Sentence length is varied. (3)			
Total points out of 25			

II. Writer's Challenge

	Self	Peer	Teacher
1. One simile (1)			
2. Vivid verbs (4)			
3. Evidence of voice (5)			
Total points out of 10			

III. Writer's Evaluation

The two important things I have learned about writing descriptively are _____

_____

_____

I think these things are important to remember because_____

_____

_____

Final Assessment

Objectives: The students will write descriptive compositions in which they describe a location of particular significance to their community, town, or city that incorporates and demonstrates the skills in this unit.

Procedure

1. Begin by reading aloud the "Introduction" and "Prompt" on page 136. Review the "Prewriting Guide" as well.

2. Have the students brainstorm possible locations in their community. You may decide to have all the students describe the same place or you may give the students choices.

3. Plan a field trip or instruct the students to visit the location with their parents and use the "Observation Guide" (page 137) to take detailed notes about the location.

4. Have the students use the "Interview Worksheet" (page 138) to interview someone who is knowledgeable about the location. This can be an expert or an informed layperson.

5. Encourage the students to do research about this location if appropriate.

6. Circulate around the room and offer guidance as the students complete the "Graphic Organizer" (page 139).

7. Instruct the students to read the "Prewriting Guidelines" (page 136) and write their rough drafts using their graphic organizers to guide them.

8. Have the students complete the "Self-Revision Activity" (page 141).

9. Divide the students into pairs and have them complete the "Peer Response Activity" (page 142).

10. Have the students complete the "Proofreading Activity" (page 143).

11. Have the students use their "Self-Revision," "Peer Response," and "Proofreading" activities to write their publishable drafts of their final piece of descriptive writing.

12. Assess the final product using the "Rubric" (page 144).

Final Assessment *(cont.)*

Portfolio Piece: Have the students include a copy of their descriptive writing in their portfolios. In addition, have the students complete the "Audience Analysis Guide for Descriptive Writing" on pages 31–32 before they write their letters. After the letters are written, have the students identify three strengths in appealing to the audience.

Publishing: 1. Have the students compile their descriptions into a booklet and mail to the local historical society, town hall, or city hall for display. 2. Display a published book of the locations in local banks, libraries, and bookstores. 3. Have students volunteer to read their descriptions at a publication party at a local library or bookstore. 4. Have an "Author's Tea" and make tea, invite parents and other relatives, and have the students share their descriptions orally. 5. Have an official "Book Signing." Bind the students' descriptions into a published book and have the students sign each other's books and copies for the school library, teachers, and parents.

Technology Connection: 1. Have students create a multimedia slideshow in which they add illustrations, photographs, appropriate music, and animation to their descriptions of the significant location. 2. Have the students use a search engine to do a keyword search on the location that they described. Instruct the students to make a list of useful Web sites that could serve as resources to teachers, parents, and other students in the community about this location.

Home-School Connection: Sponsor a "Town Meeting" at your school. At this event, have students inform community members about preserving locations that are special and important to the community.

Assessment: Use the "Rubric for Evaluating the Final Assessment" on page 144 to assess the students' descriptive writing. Allow the students an opportunity to complete the "self" column and assess their own abilities to fulfill the requirements of the assignment. Also, provide the students with an opportunity to complete the "peer" column on the rubric. Divide the students into pairs and have them give each other feedback on the eight essential elements that they must include in their descriptive writing.

Final Assessment *(cont.)*

Checklist for Success

Directions: Read the following checklist and use these guidelines to create a descriptive piece of writing that is polished and publishable.

❏ Read the Introduction and Prompt. Skim the "Prewriting Guidelines" (page 136).

❏ Use the "Observation Guide" (Page 137) to gather details about the location that you are going to be describing.

❏ Use the "Interview Worksheet" (page 138) to gather information from someone who is knowledgeable about the location that you are going to be describing.

❏ Organize your ideas using the "Graphic Organizer for Descriptive Writing" (page 139).

❏ Use the "Writer's Challenge" (page 140) to select the descriptive writing elements that you are going to incorporate into your description.

❏ Go back and reread the "Prewriting Guidelines" (page 136).

❏ Write a rough draft.

❏ Complete the "Self-Revision Activity" (page 141).

❏ Complete the "Peer-Response Activity" (page 142).

❏ Complete the "Proofreading Questions" (page 143).

❏ Write the final draft.

❏ Use the "Final Assessment Rubric" (page 144) to evaluate your final piece of descriptive writing.

Final Assessment *(cont.)*

Introduction: Your task is to describe a setting in your community, town, or city that evokes a sense of pride. This setting may be a park, a monument, a historical site, a garden, the home of a famous person, a bridge, a church, a battleground, or a nature reserve. There are several other possibilities, but the most important thing is that you choose a location that makes you feel proud to part of your community. Use the prompt below to guide you in writing your descriptive composition.

Prompt

Begin by observing this special location carefully. Write a description of this location; and in your writing, be sure to include details about landscaping, atmosphere, features of historical significance, and any evidence of wildlife. Incorporate into your description information about powerful, intriguing, sad, or joyous moments that can be associated with this location. Make sure to carefully plan your writing and then read the "Prewriting Guide" below so that you include all of the basic elements of descriptive writing when you begin drafting.

Prewriting Guidelines

As you draft your descriptive writing, remember to:

❏ Focus your topic.

❏ Write an engaging lead that "grabs" the reader.

❏ Include sufficient supporting details.

❏ Write a powerful conclusion.

❏ Show an awareness of audience.

❏ Link your ideas by using transitions.

❏ Vary your sentence structure and length.

Final Assessment *(cont.)*

Observation Guide

Directions: Observe the location that you have identified carefully and record your observations in the spaces below.

Subject being observed: _____

Date: _____

Time of day or night: _____

Purpose for observation: _____

Observe the subject carefully and record details that appeal to your senses in the chart below.

Sight	Sound	Smell	Touch	Taste

Emotional reaction to the subject: _____

_____

_____

Final Assessment *(cont.)*

Interview Worksheet

Directions: Use the following worksheet to interview an expert on the topic about which you will be writing your descriptive composition.

Location: _____

1. What makes you an authority on this location? _____

2. What are some specific sensory details that can describe this location? _____

   _____

   _____

   _____

3. Could you show me an example or tell me a story to illustrate what you know about the location?

   _____

   _____

   _____

   _____

4. What fascinates you the most about this topic? _____

   _____

   _____

   _____

5. Do you think my audience will share your fascination? Why or why not? _____

   _____

   _____

6. How did you learn all of the information about this location? _____

   _____

   _____

   _____

Final Assessment *(cont.)*

Graphic Organizer for Descriptive Writing

Directions: Use the following graphic organizer to plan your writing.

Lead: (must grab the reader's interest)

Subtopic #1:

Supporting Details:

Subtopic #2:

Supporting Details:

Subtopic #3:

Supporting Details:

Concluding Ideas: (Insightful and powerful)

Final Assessment *(cont.)*

Writer's Challenge for the Final Assessment

Directions: From the list below, select six elements of descriptive writing to incorporate into your description of a location that is meaningful in your community. Remember, you must incorporate the elements identified on the "Prewriting Guidelines" (page 136). You get choices when it comes to the elements listed below.

❏ Alliteration

❏ Assonance

❏ Repetition

❏ Onomatopoeia

❏ Hyperbole

❏ Simile

❏ Metaphor

❏ Personification

❏ Descriptive adjectives

❏ Specific nouns

❏ Vivid verbs

❏ Evidence of theme

❏ Evidence of writer's voice

❏ Tone

❏ Mood

❏ Prepositional phrases

❏ Evidence of careful observation

❏ Rhetorical question

❏ "Imagine that . . ." sentence beginning

When writing about a special location, which three elements of descriptive writing would be especially important to incorporate? Why? _____

_____

_____

_____

_____

Final Assessment *(cont.)*

Self-Revision Activity for the Final Assessment

Part I

Directions: Reread your descriptive writing carefully. As you read, complete the following exercises.

- ❏ Underline a compelling sentence from your lead.
- ❏ Circle your subtopics.
- ❏ Number your supporting details for each subtopic.
- ❏ Put a zigzag line under transitions.
- ❏ Revise any part of your descriptive writing that is weakly developed.

Part II

Directions: Respond to the following questions in order to double-check that you have included some of the necessary elements in your descriptive writing.

1. How could my lead be more interesting?

   _____

   _____

   _____

   _____

   _____

2. How could I improve my supporting details?

   _____

   _____

   _____

   _____

   _____

3. What could I add to my conclusion to make it more powerful and insightful?

   _____

   _____

   _____

   _____

   _____

Final Assessment *(cont.)*

Peer-Response Activity for the Final Assessment

Writer: _____

Peer Responder: _____

Directions: Writers read their drafts aloud to peers. When they are finished reading, writers should take notes in the space provided under each peer response question.

1. What is the location I have chosen to describe? How do you know?

   _____

   _____

   _____

2. How could my lead be more engaging to the reader? _____

   _____

   _____

3. What are the details in my writing? How could my details more clearly describe the location I have chosen?

   _____

   _____

   _____

4. What information do I need to add, delete, or change in my conclusion in order to make it more powerful?

   _____

   _____

   _____

5. How have I shown an understanding of the audience? Give specific information from the text.

   _____

   _____

   _____

6. Do I have varied sentence structure and length? Give specific examples.

   _____

   _____

   _____